Principles of accounting and finance

Principles of accounting and finance provides a comprehensive overview for managers who need to know how to obtain and use financial information effectively. It explains all the key accounting procedures, showing how to prepare statements and interpret them.

Peter Sneyd first outlines the scope and purpose of annual financial reports focusing on the principles and mechanisms of their analysis. He then looks at the management use of financial information and explains how product costs are determined, how financial information should be used for various types of decisions and how budgets are used for control purposes in order to achieve strategic objectives. The book offers the most up to date analysis of the recent developments in accounting reporting, including a detailed consideration of cash flow reports. It also discusses the impact of inflation on financial reports and the importance of cash management. Each chapter offers a step by step explanation followed by a detailed illustration of the topic concerned; a focused case study provides a context for self-assessment exercises.

The book builds an all-round picture of the issues involved, showing that there are often several solutions to any one problem and that the choice depends on accurate analysis of the specific demands of the situation at the time. By looking at the sorts of problems a manager encounters, this book offers a sound base on which to make successful financial decisions.

Peter Sneyd is Senior Lecturer in Accounting at the Manchester Metropolitan University and is a tutor for the Open University. He has wide industrial and professional experience, is a fellow of the Chartered Association of Certified Accountants and has a masters degree in accounting and finance.

Routledge series in the principles of management
Edited by Joseph G. Nellis

The Routledge series in the principles of management offers stimulating approaches to the core topics of management. The books relate the key areas to strategic issues in order to help managers solve problems and take control. By encouraging readers to apply their own experiences, the books are designed to develop the skills of the all-round manager.

Principles of marketing
G. Randall

Principles of financial management
Keith Ward and Keith Parker

Principles of information systems management
John Ward

Principles of law
A. Ruff

Principles of applied statistics
M. Fleming and J. Nellis

Principles of human resource management
D. Goss

Principles of operations management
R. L. Galloway

Principles of accounting and finance

Peter Sneyd

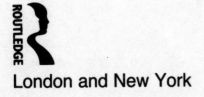

London and New York

First published 1994
by Routledge
11 New Fetter Lane, London EC4P 4EE

Simultaneously published in the USA and Canada
by Routledge
29 West 35th Street, New York, NY 10001

© 1994 Peter Sneyd

Typeset in Times by Florencetype Ltd, Kewstoke, Avon

Printed and bound in Great Britain by
Mackays of Chatham PLC, Chatham, Kent

British Library Cataloguing in Publication Data

A catalogue record for this book is available from the British Library

ISBN 0–415–07932–2

Library of Congress Cataloging in Publication Data
Sneyd, Peter.
    Principles of accounting and finance / Peter Sneyd.
        p.   cm.
    Includes bibliographical references and index.
    ISBN 0–415–07932–2
    1. Managerial accounting.   2. Corporations—Finance.   I. Title.
    HF5657.4.S57   1994
657—dc20   93–44753
                                                                         CIP

To my parents

Contents

Figures

Tables

Series editor's preface

In recent years there has been a dramatic increase in management development activity in most Western countries, especially in Europe. This activity has extended across a wide spectrum of training initiatives, from continuing studies programmes of varying durations for practising managers to the provision of courses leading to the award of professional and academic qualifications. With regard to the latter the most prominent developments have been in terms of the Master of Business Administration (MBA) and Diploma in Management (DMS) programmes, particularly in the UK where virtually every university now offers some form of post-graduate and/or post-experience management qualification.

However, the explosion of formal management training programmes such as the MBA and DMS has tended to be in advance of suitably tailored management textbooks. Many of the core functional areas of these programmes have had to rely on some of the more specialized and thus more narrowly focused textbooks, which are more appropriate for undergraduate requirements. They have generally not provided a suitable balance between academic rigour and practical, business-related relevance. The Routledge series covering the principles of management has been specifically developed to service the needs of an expanding management audience. The series deals with the full range of core subjects as well as many of the more popular elective courses that one would expect to find in most MBA and DMS programmes. Many of the books will also be attractive to those students taking professional exams, for example in accountancy, banking, etc., as well as managers attending a wide range of development courses. Each book in the series is written in a concise format covering the key principles of each topic in a pragmatic style which emphasizes the balance between theory and application. Case studies, exercises and references for further reading are provided where appropriate.

It gives me pleasure to express my thanks to the staff of Routledge for the commitment and energy which they have devoted to the development of this series, and in particular to Francesca Weaver who has skilfully steered each book through the minefield of production from beginning to end. I would also like to express my gratitude to my secretary Christine Williams for maintaining her joviality throughout the development of the 'Principles' series.

Joseph G. Nellis
Cranfield School of Management

Preface

For far too long, accountancy has been shrouded in an unnecessary mystique – what is in essence a relatively simple discipline has been presented as the prerogative of the modern-day financial witch-doctor. This is incorrect; none of the concepts utilised by the accountancy profession are beyond the comprehension and ability of any person who is of reasonable intelligence.

Accountancy is called the language of business. This is because measures of success and failure are expressed in financial terms. The result is that managers who are fluent in the language are better placed to take the correct strategic decisions.

Knowledge of the basics of accountancy is especially useful for owners and managers of smaller businesses which do not have the luxury of employing their own financial experts. Such businesses are particularly vulnerable to failure when there is a poor appreciation of their current financial state, and when those taking the decisions do not fully comprehend the consequences of their intended actions. It is equally important for managers in larger organisations to have this knowledge. As careers develop, then increasingly decisions are required that have important financial consequences. They may, for example, become budget-holders with responsibility for decisions regarding variances arising from their individual budget, or they may be required to evaluate alternative courses of action, all of which may have significant consequences for their firm's finances.

These responsibilities also extend to those employed in the public sector and increasingly over the past few years managers in this sector, including the National Health Service and education, have been introduced to the disciplines of financial management. It is indisputable that everyone employed in a supervisory capacity has responsibility, to a greater or lesser extent, for resources within the concern, and both they and the organisation can only benefit from increased financial skills. Furthermore the possession of such skills will contribute to and enhance their promotion prospects.

The purpose of this book is to provide a basic understanding of finance for the non-financial manager. It does not matter which type of organisation or which sector of the economy they are engaged in, because these principles are based on common structures. The same concepts and disciplines apply to small firms, public sector organisations and large diverse conglomerates. Differences are merely a matter of detail.

The important benefit that will be derived from this book is the ability to understand financial reports and to understand the basis upon which various types of decisions are made, as well as understanding the processes and benefits that arise as a result of planning and controlling business performance. Owners of small firms, as well as managers in other firms, will as a consequence be better placed both to converse with their accountants or financial colleagues, and to constructively contribute to important financial decisions.

The book is organised in two parts. First there is an explanation of the annual financial reports produced for all firms, which are also produced periodically during the year for internal control purposes. The scope and purpose of each statement is outlined and the underlying concepts upon which they are prepared explained. Then most importantly there is an introduction to the mechanics of financial statement analysis. This is the process whereby it is possible to 'read' a set of accounts and which is also an important aspect of evaluating the utility of a firm's financial plans.

The second part of the book is concerned with the internal use of financial information and explains how costs behave under different circumstances, how such information should be used for differing types of decisions, and how the cost of products and services is determined in different types of firms.

Finally, the principles are brought together in order to illustrate how financial plans (budgets) should be prepared and how these are used for control purposes. At this point it will be clear that the principles discussed are in the form of a loop and that the evaluation of a firm's plans concerns, in fact, the financial reports of the firm, except that these reports apply to an ensuing financial period.

The book aims to provide:

- an understanding of the structure of financial reports and their underlying concepts;
- the skill to read and critically analyse these reports;
- a knowledge of the manner in which costs behave under a variety of circumstances, and of their use for determining the pricing of products or services; and of the appropriate costs that should be used for a range of decisions;
- the ability to prepare budgets and to evaluate actual results in compari-

son with those plans, and to determine the cause of any divergence from the planned course of action.

The most effective use of the book can be made by regarding it as a course in finance for the non-financial manager. It will be beneficial to work through the book logically from start to finish, as some of the later chapters depend upon explanations given in the earlier part of the book. Subsequently it can be used as a reference book and utilised for revision of particular applications.

ACKNOWLEDGEMENTS

I am grateful to my colleague Sion Owen for reading the manuscript, for his helpful suggestions and most particularly, for checking all my calculations. My thanks are also due to Barbara O'Leary, Diane Stoneley and Michael West for both the considerable time and trouble they took in reading the manuscript and for their helpful comments.

Case study

INTRODUCING THE CASE STUDY

The essential elements of the key case study are presented on the following pages. They introduce the background and current situation of the case study, which concerns an actual business. Questions relating to this case are posed at the end of each chapter for self-assessment, and a summary of the accounting information pertinent to the case can be found at the end of the book and used for checking solutions.

Each point made in the text is illustrated by an example which, as far as is possible, is similar to those relating to the case study. The suggested solutions are to be considered an integral part of the learning experience and the greatest benefit will be obtained if an attempt is made to 'answer' the question before reading the suggested solutions. Because it will be derived from real life, the reader's solution may be as, or more effective than those suggested. Thus the fundamental nature of financial decisions is revealed, in that there are no 'correct' solutions, only those that are optimal under a given set of circumstances, or at a given point in time.

THE CASE STUDY

Peter French owns and manages a business which manufactures uphol-stered furniture, repairs upholstered furniture, undertakes the installation and refurbishment of public houses, restaurants and clubs, and also oper-ates a retail shop that sells both his own manufactured products, those of other manufacturers, and retails carpets and curtains.

He purchased the business some years ago and has since expanded into the markets described above. The purchase price included goodwill at a cost of £50,000 and was funded from savings and a bank loan secured on his home. This is being repaid by annual instalments of £5,000.

Sales are obtained from weekly advertisements placed in a number of local newspapers, together with other selected advertising in trade magazines. Increasingly orders are being obtained by recommendation, particularly in respect of refurbishment contracts.

Peter French rents a manufacturing unit on an industrial estate where he employs three craftsmen and two unskilled assistants, a driver and assistant and a secretary/bookkeeper. There is also a part-time cleaner/canteen assistant. When demand exceeds the capacity of the employees, who are expected to produce the equivalent of five and one half units per working week (either repair or manufacture), then production work is subcontracted to other self-employed upholsterers. The cost, per unit, of subcontract work is budgeted at £250 per unit for both repair and manufacture.

There is one full-time employee and two part-time assistants at the retail shop. There is a 50 per cent mark-up on the cost of all upholstered materials and of purchases from other manufacturers, and a mark-up of 100 per cent on the cost of the purchases of carpets and curtains.

All refurbishment contracts are completed by using subcontractors. The selling price on all contracts includes an agent's commission of 10 per cent and there is a profit margin of 10 per cent. The sub contract cost is 80 per cent of the selling price, which includes any subcontract materials.

The retail shop is on a short-term lease and a small storage warehouse leased on the industrial estate is used to store both work awaiting repair and completed work awaiting delivery to customers and to the retail outlet.

All work (including repair and manufacture) is recorded against job numbers (and material is issued to the same numbers). The budgeted material cost per unit for both repair and manufacture is £200.

Approximately 75 per cent of the industrial unit is used for manufacturing, with 10 per cent being canteen facilities and the remainder his own and the secretary's offices.

Audited accounts for the two years to 31 December 19X1 are provided in Appendix 1, and an analysis of the sales and costs for those years is also included. Details of the transactions during the year to 31 December 19X2, together with details of budgeted sales and expenditures for the year to 31 December 19X3, are added in order to provide the necessary data for exercises during the progression through the text of the book.

Stocks of manufactured goods and other goods purchased for resale are held at the retail shop; on average, these represent three months' purchases. Purchases for repair orders and for any sales of either carpets or curtains are only made in respect of orders received and no stock is held of these items.

All sales are made for immediate settlement and debtors represent prepayments in respect of rent, rates and insurances. Rent and rates are paid quarterly in advance and insurances are paid annually to 30 June. One month's credit is taken from all suppliers and craftsmen's wages are paid one week in arrears. Heating, lighting and telephone accounts are settled quarterly and accountancy charges are an annual account which is settled during the following year.

The accounts have been simplified in order to reduce unnecessary detail in the case exercises. The application of value added tax has been ignored, as has the implications of deductions from wages and salaries for taxation and national insurance contributions. The application of corporation tax has been simplified – in practice, the computation of this liability is quite complex. Accrued liabilities for holiday pay have also been ignored in the interests of simplification. All values have been rounded to the nearest hundred pounds.

The objective of the case is to provide the reader with a means of applying the principles expounded in the text to a 'real life' situation, without having to consider what are mainly technical details of accounting.

All the accounting information pertinent to the case is summarised in an appendix at the end of the book, and those parts relevant to particular exercises at the end of each chapter are reproduced with the exercises.

Part I

Financial reports

Chapter 1

Introduction

FINANCIAL REPORTS

All firms need to prepare and publish three annual financial statements. These comprise:

1 profit and loss account;
2 balance sheet;
3 cash flow report.

These can be used to answer three vital questions:

1 What profit (or loss) has been made in the period under review?
2 What capital is employed in the business, and how has it been raised?
3 What cash has been received by the business during the period, and how has it been spent?

The three statements reveal:

- **Profit and loss account** This reports sales and the cost of those sales, whenever incurred, as well as the overheads arising during the period under review and the profit earned for that period. It also reports on the distribution of the profit to lenders by way of loan interest, to government by way of taxation, to shareholders by way of dividends and, finally, the amount of the profit that has been retained in the business to finance further expansion and growth.
- **Balance sheet** This is a snapshot of the firm's financial position at the date of the balance sheet and records the book (cost) value of assets and liabilities of the business.
- **Cash flow report** This records the receipts and payments during the period and the effect of these transactions on the firm's liquid (cash) resources.

Before any attempt is made to understand how the financial reports can answer these questions, it is necessary to understand how business is financed and why profit is important in a business.

SOURCE AND INVESTMENT OF CAPITAL

Business activity is primarily related to risk; the raising of capital from various sources and its investment in profit-earning capacity. The risk inherent in such a situation concerns whether the return (profit) will be sufficient to repay the providers of capital and to leave a surplus that can be utilised in the business in order to expand its activities.

It will also be necessary to consider the question of how much profit is satisfactory for this purpose and, additionally, how much is needed to provide for the replacement of the original capital utilised in earning the profit when the cost of the replacement investment has increased above the original cost, i.e. as a consequence of inflation.

Capital is provided from three sources:

1 **Shareholders**   The owners of the business.
2 **Lenders**   Banks and other financial institutions.
3 **Profit**   The increase in the wealth of the business.

The characteristics of loan and share capital are different:

- Loan capital has a fixed (or determinable) rate of interest and requires repayment at a future date.
- Share capital is never repaid; once subscribed, it remains in the business permanently, and the rate of return (i.e. dividend) is determined by the profitability of the business. The individual shareholders in a firm dispose of their shares by selling them to other parties.

The capital employed in the business is invested (by the management) into two distinct categories of assets:

1 Long-term assets, e.g. property and plant in order to provide the facilities for manufacture of its products or the provision of its services. A feature of this category of investment is that, although long-term, it will require replacement, due to use, in the future.
2 Short-term investment in stocks and debtors (the provision of credit to customers). This is essentially short-term, because it is constantly being consumed and replenished. A further source of capital to the business is the short-term credit extended by suppliers. Thus the investment by the firm, in this area, is offset by the provision of this source of finance.

These principles can be illustrated as shown in Table 1.1.

It will be self-evident that the total net assets must always be the same as the capital employed, as the one arises as the result of the other.

The statement of source and investment of capital represents a simple balance sheet.

Table 1.1 Source and investment of capital

	£000	
Capital employed:		
Share capital	100	
Reserves	50	150
Loan capital		50
		200
Long-term assets		150
Short-term assets	100	
Less short-term credit	(50)	50
Total net assets		200

It will be evident that the 'assets' (i.e. things owned) are equal to the liabilities (amounts owed) of the business and in this context it is important to understand that the 'owners' (shareholders) of the business are creditors in the same manner as ordinary suppliers of materials for resale to the business. They have lent moneys (capital) to the business, and in the event of the firm being 'wound up' (i.e. ceasing to trade) while it was still solvent, they would be entitled to the return of their capital together with any undistributed profits. Thus the value of the shareholders' funds in the balance sheet is shown as the total of subscribed ordinary capital and undistributed profit.

The business has a separate legal identity to that of the shareholders owning that business, and their (the shareholders') liabilities to the other creditors of the business is limited. Hence the description of 'limited liability company'.

FLOW OF FUNDS

It is very important to understand the nature of profit and the way in which this is retained (or 'ploughed back') in business activity. Consider the balance sheet set out in Table 1.2 and the effect that the transactions arising on the day after its preparation would have on its values.

The transactions arising during the day are:

1 Purchase of materials:
   — increase in stocks;
   — increase in creditors.
2 Payment to suppliers:

Table 1.2 Effect of transactions on the balance sheet

	Day 1		Day 2	
	£	£	£	£
Share capital	100		100	
Retained profit	50	150	60	160
Loan capital		50		50
Capital employed		200		210
Plant & equipment		150		140
Stocks	50		60	
Debtors	45		60	
Cash	5		10	
	100		130	
Creditors	(50)		(60)	
		50		70
Total assets		200		210

    — decrease in cash;
    — decrease in creditors.
3 Sales to customers:
    — decrease in stocks;
    — increase in debtors.
4 Receipts from customers:
    — decrease in debtors;
    — increase in cash.
5 'Wearing out' (depreciation):
    — decrease in asset value of plant
    — increase in working capital.

It is important to understand:

1 that profit is 'earned' and reinvested each time a delivery is made to a customer, but
2 that it is not available for use in the business until the customer settles the account.

The inflow and outflow of cash in a business can be illustrated by reference to Figure 1.1, which depicts capital employed as being a tank into which flow subscriptions of share capital, loan capital and of profit. Profit arises from the investment of the capital employed into first, long-term fixed assets, which depreciate (i.e. lose value) over time, and this loss becomes

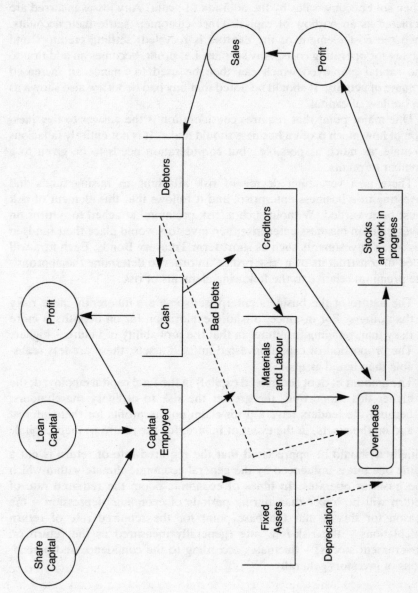

Figure 1.1 Flows of capital, cash and profit

part of the cost of production as work-in-progress. Second, into the short-term investment in stocks and work-in-progress, this investment being offset by the use of short-term creditor finance. The addition of other operating costs converts the work-in-progress into finished goods which when sold become sales by the addition of profit. Any losses incurred are depicted as an outflow of capital. Once customers settle their accounts, then the cost element of the debtors is recycled, settling creditors and paying for operating costs. Any surplus, i.e. profit, becomes an addition to the capital employed which can then be used to finance an increased volume of activity. It should be noted that any bad debts are also shown as an outflow of capital.

One major point that requires consideration is the answer to the question of how much profit a business should make. It is not entirely fallacious to state 'as much as possible', but consideration needs to be given to a number of points.

There is a very high degree of risk attaching to raising funds and investing in a business enterprise, and it follows that this element of risk must be rewarded. Without such a 'risk premium' attached to returns on investment in business enterprise then investors would place their funds in 'risk-free' investments such as short-term Treasury Bonds. Each firm will need to construct its own 'risk profile' in order to determine the appropriate premium relative to the following elements of risk:

1 The nature of the business enterprise; some are inherently more risky than others. For instance, offshore exploration for oil deposits is more risky than retailing furniture, in that the probability of failure is higher.
2 The proportion of capital invested in fixed assets; these are less realisable than liquid assets.
3 The amount of debt (borrowed capital) in the total capital employed; the higher this proportion, the greater the risk to ordinary shareholders, because the lenders have a prior claim on the profits for their interest and on the assets, in the event of failure, for the return of their capital.

Finally it should be appreciated that the required rate of return is not a static one but is influenced by the general economic climate within which the business operates. In times of economic boom the required rate of return will be lower than during periods of economic depression – the reason for this is that the base point for the required rate of return calculations – the risk-free rate (generally measured as the return on government stocks) – fluctuates according to the confidence and perceptions of investors generally.

ACCOUNTING RECORDS

The previously mentioned reports are compiled from records that are maintained by a system that has been developed to cope with differing types of transactions:

- The ownership of assets – plant, premises, moneys due from customers and unused stocks.
- Liabilities – moneys due to suppliers, lenders and to the owners of the business.
- Revenues and costs – sales, purchases of materials and the payment of expenses.

The system is known as the double-entry system of bookkeeping and it is also self-checking in order to achieve arithmetic accuracy. It was first described by Pacioli in 1494 and remains unchanged to the present day, its principles forming the basis for computerised accounting programs.

Each transaction is recorded twice, once as a debit entry and once as a credit entry. Debits are entered on the left-hand side of the ledger and credits on the right-hand side. Debit entries represent expenditure on assets or expenses, and credit entries represent income and receipts, as well as liabilities due to third parties. Therefore at the end of any accounting period the totals of all debit and credit entries will be the same and the books will 'balance', because of the 'doubling' of each entry (i.e. they are entered twice).

Most bookkeeping systems include the following records:

- Sales and purchases day-books which summarise any sales or purchases that are made on credit.
- A cash-book which records transactions made via the bank account or in cash. Most firms utilise a petty cash-book, which is a subset of the main cash-book.
- Personal ledgers for customers and suppliers, recording the amounts owed to, or by, suppliers and customers.
- A general or nominal ledger which contains the accounts for assets, liabilities, sales and expenditure, suitably classified according to the nature of the transactions.

When the accounts are closed at the end of a period, a 'trial balance' can be produced which will have the same totals for both debits and credits. The financial reports are compiled from this document, after making any adjustments that are necessary in respect of outstanding transactions.

There is no need for managers to have anything more than a general appreciation of the background to the records – it is more important that they appreciate the content and format of the specific financial reports and understand the importance of the

entries that these contain. A thorough understanding of the limitations of such reports is far more important than any expertise in account preparation.

ACCOUNTING RULES

The preparation of the financial statements involve the application of accounting conventions, or rules. These are the principles which are applied by accountants when preparing financial reports. Such statements are issued by the Accounting Standards Board in the form of edicts on the main points of account preparation. Since the early 1970s these have taken the form of 'Statements of Standard Accounting Practice' (SSAPs), some of which concern very technical points of account preparation. Since 1991 these have been superseded by Financial Reporting Standards (FRSs). Without dwelling on the finer points, the manager does need to have a broad understanding of the following main conventions:

1 **Going concern convention**   This states that the preparer can assume that the firm will continue into the future to an indefinite date. Such a rule enables a long view to be taken of certain types of transaction, namely the ownership of assets.
2 **Conservatism**   This essentially requires that a prudent view is taken of profit and that profit is never anticipated, even when the amount is known with certainty. On the other hand, where a loss is suspected then a provision for that loss will be made even though the amount of the loss cannot be ascertained with any accuracy. This rule effectively means that profits will always be reported at the lowest amount and no anticipation of profit is made, whereas all foreseen losses have been taken into account.

   To some extent the going concern convention represents a relaxation of this rule, in that for certain transactions losses are not recorded. For example, if a firm buys machinery that they expect to last ten years then under the going concern rule it can be written off over the anticipated useful life. Under the conservatism rule, however, any potential loss on the sale of that plant, in its used condition, ought to be recorded at the date the accounts are prepared.
3 **Realisation**   Profits are only reported after they have been realised. That is, the profit on the sale of goods is only recorded when those goods have been delivered to the customer. Thus this rule underpins that of conservatism.
4 **Matching**   When calculating the profit for a period, the calculation is made by 'matching' the sales of the period with those costs incurred in making those sales. In the event that a firm has incurred costs which have not resulted in a sale, then they are disregarded for the purpose of calculating the profit for that period. In effect, if a firm purchases goods

for resale and does not sell them during the accounting period, then the cost of those goods is not deducted in the calculation of the profit for that period. The cost is treated as an investment for the future and is recorded on the balance sheet.

5 **Accruals** Income and expenditure that arises in respect of a period of time, e.g. insurance premiums or rents, are deemed to 'accrue' on a day-to-day basis, for the purpose of profit calculation. This enables any transactions that overlap two accounting periods to be split into the respective periods that they refer to in the appropriate proportions.

6 **Cost** This is a very important convention, which requires that all transactions are recorded, and reported, at their historic cost, that is the value at the time of the transaction. This means that any value shown in a financial report is the cost value and is not intended to be representative of its market value. For example, the value of fixed assets in the balance sheet is their cost less any amounts that have been written off in respect of reduction in value due to use. They are not either the resale value of those assets, nor are they the value of replacing those assets.

7 **True and fair view** Whatever the effect of the application of the above rules, or of the many others, the overall effect must be that the financial reports show a true and fair view of the financial position of the firm at the date of the reports.

KEY LEARNING POINTS

- **The scope and content of the financial reports has been described; each will be considered separately in subsequent chapters.**
- **An explanation of the sources of capital to a firm, and the manner in which this capital is invested and illustrated in the form of a balance sheet has been given.**
- **An illustration of the flow of funds into and out of a business, reflecting the essentially dynamic nature of business activity, has been supplied.**
- **A summary and brief description of the main accounting records that a firm needs to maintain has been provided.**
- **A definition has been set out of the main accounting conventions that are applied in the preparation of financial reports, all of which will be illustrated in the chapters on the individual financial reports.**

CASE STUDY

1 Consider the books of account and other records that will be necessary to the business described in the case study. What details will be necessary in order to prepare periodic reports that will enable effective control to be exercised?

2 Consider the effect of applying the accounting conventions discussed in this chapter on the accounts for the year to 31 December 19X1. Identify examples of each of the conventions discussed.

Chapter 2

Profit statements

INTRODUCTION

The function of this report is to calculate the profit earned on the sales during the period. Adoption of the matching principle means that the costs deducted may not have have arisen during the period covered by the report, but may have been 'allocated' to that period, even though they may have been incurred in a previous period. At one extreme this could result in costs being deducted, in the computation of profit for a given period, that may have arisen in a number of different time periods. During periods of rapidly changing prices (inflation) this can give rise to problems in the interpretation of financial reports.

The Companies Act 1989 requires a specific format to be adopted for the presentation of profit and loss accounts. This is shown in Table 2.1. Where information is not disclosed in detail in the published report, then the details must be revealed in the notes to the accounts. Turnover must show an analysis by class of business (and give details of profit before taxation for each class) and also by geographical spread.

The amounts for distributive and administrative costs must be shown separately. Details of 'other operating income' must be given, as must income from fixed asset investments. Amounts written off fixed asset investments will consist primarily of the depreciation provision for the year. 'Interest payable' must distinguish the interest payable on loans over five years from interest payable on loans repayable under five years, and must also show a further distinction between the interest payable on those loans repayable by instalments, and the interest on those loans not so repayable.

Additional information to be disclosed in the notes to the accounts is as follows:

- Auditors' remuneration.
- Payments for the hire of plant.
- Details of directors' remuneration.
- Details of employees' remuneration, showing:

Table 2.1 Formal profit and loss account

Profit and loss account for the year ended 31 December 19X1

	Notes	19X1 £	19X0 £
Turnover	–	x	x
Cost of sales		x	x
Gross profit		x	x
Distribution and administrative cost	–	x	x
		x	x
Other operating income	–	x	x
Operating income		x	x
Income from fixed asset investment	–	x	x
		x	x
Amounts written off investments	–	x	x
		x	x
Interest payable	–	x	x
Profit on ordinary activities before taxation		x	x
Taxation	–	x	x
Profit after taxation, before extraordinary items		x	x
Extraordinary items	–	x	x
Profit for year		x	x
Dividends	–	x	x
Retained profit for year		x	x

— wages and salaries;
— social security costs;
— other pension provisions;
— details of average numbers employed.

'Extraordinary items' are defined by FRS 3 as those items which derive from events or transactions outside the usual activities of the business, that are both material and not expected to recur regularly. They are not items that are exceptional by virtue of their value. FRS 3 also covers the treatment of prior year adjustments, which are defined as those arising from either of:

1 changes in accounting policies;
2 fundamental errors.

Again, the values must be material.

Although the rate of corporation tax is 35 per cent, it should not be assumed that this will be based on the figure for profit on ordinary activities. In order to compute the liability for taxation it is necessary to exclude certain types of expenses and depreciation, and to make deduction for any allowances for the purchase of plant or buildings.

Dividends are the total of both interim dividends paid during the year and the final dividend proposed by the directors in respect of the profit shown for the year. The total dividend requires approval by the shareholders at the annual general meeting called to approve the accounts. It is interesting to note that it is well established in English law that shareholders can reduce proposed dividends, but cannot increase them.

The operating profits shown in the above statement represent the earnings on the capital employed in the business. It is from this fund that the lenders are paid interest; taxation is then assessed on the remaining profits. The profits after taxation has been deducted represent the earnings available to the ordinary shareholders, who are the owners of the business, and who are the 'risk-takers' providing the necessary capital for the business and being dependent on the level of after-tax profits for their reward. The directors decide how much of the earnings are to be distributed as dividends; their decision will be influenced by a number of factors, such as the need to maintain liquidity, the immediate investment programme in fixed assets and, importantly, the need to maintain a regular flow of dividends. The remaining profit is that which has been reinvested in the assets of the business. This has already been reinvested on each occasion that a sale has been made to a customer.

MANAGEMENT PROFIT STATEMENTS

The above format for the profit statement is that which is published; for internal management control purposes, however, a much more detailed format will be required, which will not contain any entries for taxation, dividends or extraordinary items. The format will reflect the individual requirements and characteristics of the particular firm. The example provided in Table 2.2 may be illustrative. SSAP 9 requires the valuation of stocks and work-in-progress at the lower of cost or net realisable value and it will be readily appreciated that this will involve the exercise of judgement. Additionally the valuation of stocks may require the resolution, by judgement, of the following questions:

● the extent of the physical verification of quantities;
● the choice of a conversion rate for purchases made in foreign currencies;

Table 2.2 Internal management profit statement

Trading and profit and loss account for the year ended 31 December 19X1

	£000	
	£	£
Sales		200
Stocks 1 January 19X1	30	
Purchases	120	
	150	
Less stocks 31 December 19X1	40	
Materials used	110	
Wages	40	
Cost of sales		150
Gross profit		50
Salaries	10	
Rent and rates	5	
Heating etc.,	2	
Insurances	3	
Advertising	6	
Motor expenses	3	
Sundries	1	
Bad and doubtful debts	2	
Depreciation	3	35
Operating profit		15
Less interest		3
Net profit before tax		12
Taxation		4
Net profit after tax		8
Dividends		4
Retained profit		4

- the future usability of stock items, due to technical obsolescence or deterioration;
- the adoption of cost accounting methodology to determine the production overheads that are to be included in the work-in-progress and finished goods valuations.

The fact that judgement is required means that the computation of profit is not a mechanistic exercise, but one that is influenced, to a greater or lesser extent, by subjectivity. The extent to which this applies will depend on the significance of the items subject to the above considerations, and on the relationship between their values and the amount of profit. However, as it is not unusual for stock valuations to be several times the value of profits, acceptable margins in the valuation of stocks may become unacceptable variations in the amount of profit. For example an acceptable margin of +/− 5 per cent in stock valuation would become an unacceptable margin of +/− 25 per cent where the value of stock was five times greater than that of profit. This illustration is not an implied criticism of the principles of account preparation, but a necessary process in order to conform to the prevalent accounting conventions.

The foregoing illustration demonstrates the application of the matching principle where it shows the purchases of materials being adjusted for the opening and closing stock values. Those purchases made during the period, but not sold or used, are carried forward until they can be 'matched' against the sales that they create.

The accruals principle is not illustrated, but the expenses deducted for the period are those relevant to the period, regardless of whether or not an invoice has been received. In the event that an account is received for a period longer than that under review, then the appropriate proportion is carried forward to a subsequent period(s).

The provision for bad and doubtful debts illustrates the application of the convention of conservatism. This item will contain provision for any debts that management feels may become bad in the future. This is a further illustration of the application of subjective judgement in the computation of profit.

The calculation of the depreciation provision is the result of the application of the going concern principle. A further example of this (not illustrated) is the treatment of research and development expenditure. Any firm that incurs expense on the research into, and development of, products for sale in future periods can, under both the matching principle and the going concern principle, carry that expenditure forward to future periods until the sales income from those expenditures arises. Such a treatment calls for the exercise of judgement of the highest order. In order to constrain the exercise of such judgement, SSAP 13 was issued which requires that:

1 expenditure on pure and applied research is written off in the period in which is it incurred;
2 development expenditure is written off in the year in which it is incurred, unless there is a clearly defined project whose outcome can be assessed with certainty.

If nothing else, the SSAP ensures that the application of conservatism overrides that of the matching or going concern principles which could

Table 2.3 Data for preparation of profit and loss account

	£000
Sales	200
Purchases	
(NB materials are 40% of sales)	90
Stocks on hand 1 January 19X1	30
Wages	20
Salaries	10
Administration overheads	25
Selling and distribution overheads	20
Depreciation: 10% per annum on fixed	
assets costing £100,000	
Interest on loans	5
Taxation 30%	
Dividends 10p per share	
(issued capital 100,000	
£1 shares)	

result in expenditure on unfruitful research being carried forward to be written off in future periods. The resulting profit statement is shown in Table 2.4.

The profit statement reflects the accepted layout, and the cost of materials used is calculated at 40 per cent of sales with the stocks at 31 December being calculated as the difference between this figure (£80,000) and the total of the opening stock and the purchases. Overheads have been shown as administration and selling and distribution, in order to reduce detail.

The application of appropriate accounting conventions can be illustrated by incorporating adjustments into the profit statement in respect of the following circumstances:

1 £5,000 of stock is considered unsaleable.
2 Yearly insurance premiums of £10,000 are included in 'administration overheads' and expire in June 19X2.
3 £3,000 of debtors are considered doubtful (and should be included in 'selling and distribution overheads').
4 An additional loan for £100,000 (at 10 per cent per annum interest) was taken out on 1 July 19X1 and no interest has been paid, nor has a reserve been made in the profit statement.
5 A bonus of £5,000 is to be paid, in March 19X2, to salaried staff, in respect of the year to 31 December 19X1.

After redrafting the profit statement, as shown in Table 2.5, to incorporate the above, consideration can be given to the effect that they would have on the entries in the balance sheet.

Table 2.4 Profit and loss account

Trading and profit and loss account, year ending 31 December 19X1

	£000	
	£	£
Sales		200
Stocks, 1 January 19X1	30	
Purchases	90	
	120	
Less stocks, 31 December 19X1	40	
Materials used	80	
Wages	20	
Cost of sales		100
Gross profit		100
Salaries	10	
Administration overheads	25	
Selling and distribution overheads	20	
Depreciation	10	65
Operating profit		35
Less interest		5
Net profit before tax		30
Taxation		9
Net profit after taxation		21
Dividends		10
Retained profit		11

The reduction of the stock valuation at the year end reflects the conservatism convention which recognises loss at the earliest possible moment. In the event that the stock was sold at a later date then all of the sale proceeds would be included in the profit statement at that point. The accruals convention is illustrated by the reduction of administrative overheads to disallow that proportion of the insurance premium that relates to the next accounting period, and the charge for salaries is increased to include the bonus that will be paid in March of the following year. The amount of this bonus would not be determined until after the year end when the amount of profit was calculated but, nevertheless, under this convention a charge would be made in the accounts for the year to which it relates. Similar comments apply to the provision for loan interest. The

Table 2.5 Amended profit and loss account

Trading and profit and loss account for the year ended 31 December 19X1

	£000	
	£	£
Sales		200
Stocks, 1 January 19X1	30	
Purchases	90	
	120	
Less stocks, 31 December 19X1	35	
Materials used	85	
Wages	20	
Cost of sales		105
Gross profit		95
Salaries	15	
Administration overheads	20	
Selling and distribution overheads	23	
Depreciation	10	68
Operating profit		27
Less interest		10
Net profit before taxation		17
Taxation		5
Net profit after taxation		12
Dividends		10
Retained profit		2

provision for bad and doubtful debts reflects the conservatism principle, and the loss arising from potential (or perceived) bad debts is recorded at the earliest possible moment.

The previous adjustments would also need to be adjusted on the balance sheet. A summary of those would be as shown in Table 2.6.

ILLUSTRATION

Table 2.7 provides a summary of the receipts and payments of a firm for the year ended 30 June 19X9. From the above information it is possible to prepare a profit and loss account, balance sheet and cash flow report for the year to 30 June 19X9.

Table 2.6 Summary of profit statement adjustments

				£
1	Stocks		less	5,000
	Reserves		less	5,000
2	Debtors	(prepayments)	add	5,000
	Reserves		add	5,000
3	Debtors	(doubtful debts)	less	3,000
	Reserves		less	3,000
4	Creditors	(interest)	add	5,000
	Reserves		less	5,000
5	Creditors	(bonus)	add	5,000
	Reserves		less	5,000
6	Reduction in taxation provision:			
	Creditors		less	4,000
	Reserves		add	4,000

Note: The net effect on reserves is less £9,000 which is the difference between the two retained profit calculations.

Table 2.7 Receipts and payments

	£000
Receipts from customers	7,900
Receipt from increase in 10% loan	1,000
Payments to suppliers	3,800
Payment of salaries and wages	2,000
Payments for advertising	400
Payment of administration expenses	600
Payment of taxation	600
Payment of loan interest	100
Payment of loan instalment	200
Payment of dividends	100
Payment for new fixed assets	900

The important aspect of the illustration is not the preparation, but an understanding of the implications and consequent affect on the foregoing reports of the accounting conventions.

In order to prepare the profit and loss account, a number of adjustments need to be made to the transactions in order to reflect the accounting conventions underlying the presentation of financial reports, which will require some of the information shown in Table 2.8.

Table 2.8 Balance sheet data

		£000	
		19X8	*19X9*
Debtors		1,000	2,000
Stocks		1,000	1,500
Creditors	– Supplies	400	600
	– Taxation	600	
	– Dividends	100	
Fixed assets		10,000	
Accumulated depreciation (10% per annum straight line)		4,800	
Taxation – 25% of profit after deducting loan interest			
Dividends – distributed as 50% of profits after taxation			
Ordinary share capital		4,000	
Reserves		1,300	
Loan (10%)		1,000	

Sales

These are shown as the sales made during the period, and the receipts need to be adjusted to take account of moneys owing at the start and end of the year. The receipts will include those amounts outstanding at the commencement and will not include those owing at the end of the year. The sales for the period are therefore as shown in Table 2.9. It is important to note that the sales figure upon which profit is to be calculated is £1,000,000 more than the cash receipts.

Table 2.9 Calculation of sales

	£000
Receipts per statement	7,900
Less opening debtors	1,000
	6,900
Add closing debtors	2,000
Sales for year	8,900

Material purchases

A similar adjustment to that shown above, to reflect the materials purchased, as opposed to those paid for, is made to the payments to suppliers.

This results in a figure for purchases of £4,000,000. (The reader can check the accuracy of this calculation.)

However, the purchases are not necessarily the materials used for the sales, and in order to reflect the matching convention it is necessary to adjust the purchases figure to reflect any materials that have not been used (i.e. closing stocks) and also to take into account any stocks that have been used that were purchased the previous year, as shown in Table 2.10. Once again, notice that the value used for profit calculation is different to the figure for payments.

Table 2.10 Calculation of materials used

	£000
Material purchases	4,000
Add opening stock	1,000
	5,000
Less closing stock	1,500
Materials used	3,500

Table 2.11 Calculation of annual depreciation

	£000
Cost of fixed assets (start of year)	10,000
Additions during year	900
Total at end of year	10,900
Annual depreciation (10% straight line)	1,090

Table 2.12 Calculation of depreciation provision

	£000
Balance at start of year	4,800
Depreciation charge for year	1,090
Balance at end of year	5,890

Table 2.13 Calculation of annual loan interest costs

	£000
Loan at start of year	1,000
Add increase during year	1,000
	2,000
Interest at 10% per annum	200

Table 2.14 Profit and loss account

Profit and loss account for the year ending 30 June 19X9

	£000
Sales	8,900
Materials	3,500
Wages and salaries	2,000
Advertising	400
Administration expenses	600
Depreciation	1,090
	7,590
Operating profit	1,310
Less interest	200
Profit before taxation	1,110
Taxation (25%)	280
Profit after taxation	830
Dividends	415
Retained profit	415

In order to complete the preparation of the profit statement two further adjustments are necessary. First the annual charge for depreciation is required, and second it is necessary to provide for the interest on the loan which has accrued but which has not been paid. The first adjustment reflects the going concern convention, whereby the firm purchases fixed assets and 'recovers' the cost over the estimated useful lives of the assets. In the second case the inclusion of the interest reflects the accruals convention, whereby income and expenditure are deemed to accrue on a day-to-day basis. Therefore although payment may not yet be due, provision for the appropriate amount of interest is included in the calculation of profit.

This illustration also reflects the conservatism convention, in that losses are anticipated but profits are not.

The calculation of the charge for depreciation is shown in Table 2.11. Table 2.12 shows the treatment of the depreciation provision, on all fixed assets at the end of the year. This information is reported in the balance sheet. The loan interest cost is set out as in Table 2.13. According to the summary of transactions £100 of the loan interest has been paid, therefore the balance (£100) will be reported in the balance sheet as a creditor due within one year.

Other calculations that are required to complete the profit statement (Table 2.14) are in respect of taxation and dividends. However, as these are made in relation to items in the profit statement, they can be calculated as the report is finalised. An interesting point that will be examined in Chapter 4 is the extent to which the retained profits represent the increase in cash resources.

The preparation of the balance sheet and of the cash flow report from the above data are discussed in Chapters 3 and 4 respectively.

KEY LEARNING POINTS

- **The profit and loss account calculates the profit earned on the sales made during the financial year.**
- **Any expenses that have been incurred that relate to future sales are carried forward, on the balance sheet, as an investment for the future.**
- **The profit calculation is the subject of managerial judgement in several important areas, of which the valuation of stocks and work-in-progress is the most significant.**
- **The profit and loss account measures the earnings on the capital employed in the business, for that particular year, and reveals how this has been used to pay the interest on any loan capital and to pay taxation, as well as revealing the balance available for the ordinary shareholders and how much of this has been distributed as dividends and how much reinvested in the business for expansion.**
- **The most important values are:**
  - **sales;**
  - **operating profit;**
  - **loan interest;**
  - **profits after taxation;**
  - **dividends.**

CASE STUDY

Preparation of profit statement

Prepare a profit statement for Peter French for the year to 31 December 19X2 from the data in Table 2.15, following the same format as that shown in Table 2.4.

During the year a new car was purchased for £15,000 and the old one sold for book value. The old one had been purchased in 19X0 for £8,000. Additional plant was purchased during the year for £2,000. The car is depreciated at 25 per cent per annum by the reducing balance method, and plant is depreciated at 10 per cent per annum by the straight-line method.

Note that it is not necessary to make the adjustments for opening and closing stocks, as the figures given are for materials used. It is, however, necessary to calculate the depreciation charge for the year and it will be necessary to read Chapter 3 to find out how to make these calculations. Taxation should be provided at 25 per cent of the profit before taxation.

Dividend policy

No dividends have ever been made to the shareholders of the limited company. Although Peter French is the majority shareholder, do you think that he should establish a policy of declaring annual dividends, in the same way that an established public limited company such as Marks and Spencer's does? What do you think the advantages and disadvantages of such a policy would be to Peter French?

Table 2.15 Transactions for 19X2

During the year to 31 December 19X2 the following
transactions were entered into:

	£000
Sales	
Repair	122.2
Contract	50.0
Manufactured goods	84.2
Other goods	45.0
Carpets	27.0
Curtains	12.0
Totals	340.4
Materials	
Repairs	34.8
Contract	40.0
Manufactured goods	28.3
Other goods	30.5
Carpets	13.5
Curtains	6.0
Totals	153.1
Wages	
Craftsmen	44.6
Cleaner	3.2
Office	8.0
Shop	19.8
Totals	75.6
Subcontract	17.5
Commissions	5.0
Overheads	
Rent and rates – Unit	5.5
– Storage	1.2
– Shop	4.0
Heating and lighting – Unit	1.1
– Shop	0.9
Telephone – Unit	1.1
– Shop	0.5
Car expenses	1.8
Van expenses	2.5
Other expenses	1.5
Loan interest	6.5
Lease van	2.4
Accountancy, etc.,	2.5
Insurances	3.0
Totals	34.5
Director's salary	30.0

Chapter 3

Balance sheets

INTRODUCTION

The balance sheet is a statement of value at a given point in time (the date of the document); it has been stated that business activity is dynamic, and that the balance sheet reflects this dynamism. The publication of the document 'freezes' the values at a single point in time. The balance sheet reflects the essentially dynamic nature of business trading – each transaction that takes place during the financial period has an effect on at least two entries on the balance sheet.

The balance sheet reveals the assets and liabilities of the firm at that point in time. The assets are the resources of the firm and the liabilities are the debts (moneys owing) of the firm. In this context it should be appreciated that the capital of the firm (the moneys subscribed by the owners of the firm) is treated as a debt as the balance sheet represents the position of the firm as a separate trading organisation, distinct from its owners.

The assets comprise the long-term investment in fixed assets, which may consist of land and buildings, plant and machinery and motor vehicles, together with the shorter-term investment in working capital, which is represented by the net current assets in the balance sheet. This comprises investment in stocks of materials, work-in-progress and stocks of finished goods; investment in debtors and any cash balances. This investment is partially funded by liabilities due to shorter-term creditors – the current liabilities. The total of these investments is the capital employed in the business, which is funded from two sources: long-term loans, which bear a fixed or determinable rate of interest, and the shareholders' (owners') funds, which comprise two elements – the original capital subscribed, together with any profits made in the past which have not been distributed as dividends.

An example of the formal presentation of a balance sheet is shown in Table 3.1. The most significant figure in the document is that of 'capital employed', which is represented by the entry 'total assets less current

Table 3.1 Formal presentation of a balance sheet

Balance sheet as at 31 December 19XX		£000
	Cost depreciation	
Fixed assets		
Land & buildings	4,000	4,000
Plant & machinery	6,000	4,000	2,000
Motor vehicles	2,000	1,000	1,000
	12,000	5,000	7,000
Current assets		
Stock and work-in-progress	5,000	
Debtors	5,000	
Cash	4,000	
	14,000	
Less current liabilities		
Creditors due within one year	4,000	
Net current assets		10,000
Total assets less current liabilities		17,000
Less long-term loans		3,000
Total net assets		14,000
Financed by:		
Issued ordinary shares		10,000
Profit and loss account		4,000
Shareholders' funds		14,000

liabilities'. This shows the investment of the capital into the two significant areas – long-term investment represented by fixed assets, and the investment in working capital represented by net current assets. This latter figure is supplemented by short-term creditors to provide the funds from which the investment in stocks and debtors is made. Any difference between the amount available for investment and the actual amount of investment in these areas is represented by the cash balance, either a surplus where the actual investment is less than the funds available, or an overdraft where the investment exceeds the funds available. In this latter case the overdraft is shown as a current liability, i.e. repayable on demand.

PREPARATION

An example of the manner in which balance sheets are prepared is provided in Table 3.2, which is, in effect, an abridged trial balance, which is simply a list of the balances in the books of account at the date of the balance sheet. The object of the exercise is merely to emphasise the layout of the items in the balance sheet.

Table 3.2 Simple trial balance

	£000
Issued ordinary share capital	500
Stocks and work-in-progress	100
Creditors	120
Cash balances	370
Loan capital	500
Debtors	200
Profit and loss account	100
Plant and machinery	200
Land and buildings	400
Depreciation – plant and machinery	50

The resulting balance sheet is shown in Table 3.3. The dynamic nature of the balance sheet can be illustrated by considering the effect of the changes that will arise from a number of transactions that are completed following its date. These transactions are shown in Table 3.4. Table 3.5 shows the adjusted balance sheet after the transactions, the effects of which are summarised in Table 3.6. Consideration of the nature of these transactions reflects the principles upon which financial reports are prepared. Where the property was revalued, the revaluation reserve is shown as the appreciation from the original cost, as a gain, and included in the shareholders' funds. This is because this is a gain to that part of those funds invested in this asset. The asset may have been partially funded from the loan capital (i.e. a mortgage), but because this is to be repaid, all of the gain accrues to the ordinary shareholders.

The function of the depreciation of fixed assets reflects the application of the going concern principle which allows the view to be held that the firm will continue into the future and thus allow the cost of the asset to be recovered from sales arising from its use over its expected life.

The matching principle is illustrated by the stock values at the date of the balance sheet, which reflect purchases and expenses from which sales have not yet arisen. These are carried forward (i.e. not charged against sales in that period) to be deducted in the calculation of the profit in a future period.

The values attributed to the stocks, and also to debtors, reflect the

Table 3.3 Example of balance sheet preparation

Balance sheet		£000	
	Cost	depreciation	
Fixed assets			
Land and buildings	400		400
Plant and machinery	200	50	150
	600	50	550
Current assets			
Stocks and work-in-progress		100	
Debtors		200	
Cash		370	
		670	
Less current liabilities			
Creditors		120	
Net current assets			550
Total assets less current liabilities			1,100
Less long-term loans			500
Total net assets			600
Financed by:			
Issued ordinary shares			500
Profit and loss account			100
Shareholders' funds			600

Table 3.4 Transactions after date of balance sheet

1   Pay all the creditors.
2   Revalue land and buildings to £500,000.
3   Buy £20,000 of stock on credit.
4   Raise £40,000 by issuing ordinary shares.
5   Repay £400,000 of the loan capital.
6   Make cash sales of £100,000 at a gross profit of 25% (on cost) while maintaining stock at current levels.
7   Receive £100,000 from debtors.
8   Declare a dividend of £20,000 to the shareholders.
9   Pay 10% interest on the loan.
10 Buy a motor vehicle for £50,000 and depreciate this by 20%.

Table 3.5 Adjusted balance sheet after transactions

Balance sheet			£000
	Cost	*depreciation*	
Fixed assets			
Land and buildings	500		500
Plant and machinery	200	50	150
Motor vehicles	50	10	40
	750	60	690
Current assets			
Stocks and work-in-progress		120	
Debtors		100	
Cash		0	
		220	
Less current liabilities			
Creditors	40		
Overdraft	30	70	
Net current assets			150
Total assets less current liabilities			840
Less long-term loans			100
Total net assets			740
Financed by:			
Issued ordinary shares			540
Revaluation reserve		100	
Profit and loss account		100	200
Shareholders' funds			740

principle of conservatism in that stocks are valued at their cost, or net realisable value, where the current cost is lower than the original purchase price. 'Debtors' reflect the amounts expected to be received, and thus any bad or doubtful debts have been ignored. These are deducted from sales revenue as an expense when calculating the profit for the period.

Table 3.6 Summary of post balance sheet transactions

			£000
1	Pay all the creditors		
	Creditors	less	120
	Cash	less	120
2	Revalue land and buildings		
	Land and buildings	add	100
	Revaluation reserve	add	100
3	Buy stock on credit		
	Stocks	add	20
	Creditors	add	20
4	Issue ordinary shares		
	Share capital	add	40
	Cash	add	40
5	Repay loan capital		
	Loan capital	less	400
	Cash	less	400
6	Make cash sales and maintain stock		
	Cash	add	100
	Profit and loss	add	20
	Cash (replacement of stock)	less	80
7	Receive cash from debtors		
	Debtors	less	100
	Cash	add	100
8	Declare a dividend		
	Profit and loss	less	20
	Creditors	add	20
9	Pay interest on loan		
	Profit and loss	less	10
	Cash	less	10
10	Buy and depreciate a motor vehicle		
	Motor vehicles	add	50
	Cash	less	50
	Depreciation	add	10
	Profit and loss	less	10

CONTENTS

Table 3.7 is an illustration of a balance sheet prepared in accordance with
the requirements of the Companies Act 1989. Before discussion of the
detail of the entries contained in the balance sheet, two points are worthy
of mention: first, that there is a requirement to provide comparative figures
for the previous year, and second, to note the practice of delegating much
of the detail relating to individual entries to the notes to the accounts.
These are usually quite extensive, even for medium-sized companies, and

where a note is made then an annotation will be referenced on the balance sheet.

Intangible assets

As the description implies, these are assets that have no physical substance – patents, trade marks and goodwill. They represent costs incurred that have long-term benefits. Generally, because of their nature, these are 'written off' (i.e. deducted from reserves) and entered in the balance sheet at a nominal value to record their existence. Goodwill usually arises where assets are acquired at a value above their balance sheet value.

Tangible assets

These include land and buildings, both freehold and leasehold, plant, vehicles and other types of physical assets. Freehold land and buildings are rarely depreciated, and, on occasion, can be revalued in order that the document reflects their current value. Whatever increase is recorded is also included in the revaluation reserve and is not included in the profit arising from trading activities in that year. The remaining assets are depreciated, that is written off by instalments over their perceived useful life. The instalment written off in any particular year is deducted from the profits made on the trading activities. The entries in the balance sheet record the original cost less all depreciation written off to the date of the document.

Investments

These are shown at their cost, and a note of any market value is added where appropriate.

Stocks

These include stocks of raw materials, partly completed work and finished goods. Stocks are valued in accordance with SSAP 9, the general requirement of which is that these items shall be valued at cost, or net realisable value where this is lower. In other words, if the cost of an item has fallen since it was purchased, then the current purchase price (the market price) is used instead. This is a further illustration of the principle of conservatism, which requires that foreseeable losses shall be recorded at the earliest possible moment. This situation is quite common in industries that purchase base metals such as copper. SSAP 9 also requires that production overheads are included in the valuations of partly completed goods and finished goods. It recognises that conditions vary from industry to industry and allows for alternative methods of valuation where these are a reason-

Table 3.7 Formal balance sheet

Balance sheet as at 31 December 19X3

	Notes	19X3 £000	19X2 £000
Fixed assets			
Intangible assets	–	x	x
Tangible assets	–	x	x
Investments	–	x	x
		x	x
Current assets			
Stocks	–	x	x
Debtors	–	x	x
Cash		x	x
		x	x
Less current liabilities			
Creditors due within one year	–	x	x
Net current assets		x	x
Total assets less current liabilities		x	x
Creditors due after more than one year	–	(x)	(x)
Provisions for liabilities and charges	–	(x)	(x)
Net assets		x	x
Capital and reserves			
Called-up share capital	–	x	x
Share premium account	–	x	x
Revaluation reserve	–	x	x
Other reserves	–	x	x
Profit and loss account	–	x	x
		x	x

Note: The total of the 'capital and reserves' is equal to the total for 'net assets'

able approximation of cost. For example, in the retail industry it is common to value stocks by deducting a percentage from the retail selling price. There are occasions where the cost rule is relaxed, however, and an element for profit is included in the valuation (in contravention of the conservatism principle), such as in the case of long-term contracts. Where such a contract takes place over more than one year, then it is permissible to include some of the profits on the contract in proportion to the extent that the contract has been completed. Although this contravenes the conservatism principle, SSAP 2 (*Disclosure of Accounting Policies*) requires that the overriding convention will always be that the accounts should show a 'true and fair' view of the firms financial results.

It should, however, be recognised that 'true and fair' is an expression of the subjective opinion of the account preparer, the management, and that therein lie many of the problems that arise in the comparison of performance between firms.

Debtors

It has previously been mentioned that debtors (moneys due in respect of past sales) are shown net of actual and possible bad and doubtful debts, and it will also include expenses that have been incurred but which relate to future periods – prepayments. This is an illustration of the accruals convention, which assumes that expense accrues on a day-to-day basis. Thus where an expense is incurred that relates to a period beyond the date of the balance sheet, then that proportion relating to the future period is treated as being 'owed' by that period and is included in debtors as moneys due. An example of this type of transaction is an insurance premium which is paid in advance for a year, the anniversary of which arises after the date of the balance sheet.

Current liabilities

Current liabilities are those payable within one year, and include such items as:

- creditors for the supply of materials and expenses such as wages;
- dividends voted from the profits for the current period.

Creditors

Creditors will include 'accrued' expenses, which are the reverse of prepayments. Thus where an account is received after the date of the balance sheet which relates to the period covered by the accounts, then an entry is made in order to deduct this when computing the profits for the period. Where the amount is not known with certainty then an estimate is made.

Creditors due after more then one year will include all borrowings, whether secured or not, of whatever length of time.

Provisions for liabilities and charges

Provisions for liabilities and charges will relate mainly to taxation liabilities, including liability for deferred taxation, and to pension and similar obligations. Deferred taxation arises due to the vagaries of the United Kingdom taxation system. Allowances, against taxation liabilities, are, and have been, given annually, in respect of the purchase of certain fixed assets and when these are finally sold a liability to tax may arise in respect of the difference between the 'book' value of an asset and the sale price.

Capital and reserves

Called-up share capital is the amount received and a note is shown of the authorised share capital. This is the amount that can be issued and which must be approved by shareholders in general meeting, as must any increase in the authorised share capital. The share premium account reflects any sums received from the issue of shares above the nominal (par) value of the shares. It will be appreciated that the market value of shares fluctuates with the fortunes of the individual firm and with economic conditions generally. A revaluation reserve arises, as previously noted, when a firm revalues its fixed assets. This usually relates to the value of freehold property. 'Other reserves' will relate to those specified by the firm from its distributable profits, and the profit and loss account balance is the amount of undistributed profit made by the firm since its inception.

DEPRECIATION

In order to understand the nature of account preparation in general, and of balance sheets in particular, it is necessary to consider the treatment of depreciation in some depth.

SSAP 12 defines depreciation as a measure of wearing out, consumption or other loss of value arising from use, passage of time or obsolescence through technology or market changes. The SSAP requires that depreciation should be allocated to accounting periods so as to charge a fair proportion of an asset's cost to each period over the expected useful life of the asset.

It follows that it is necessary to:

1 Ascertain the cost of the asset.
2 Determine its useful life, giving due regard to anticipated changes in technology or market requirements.
3 Estimate the probable sale value at the end of the perceived useful life. It is recognised that this is a difficult matter; where the value is

considered to be small in relation to the cost, it is recommended that it is treated as nil.

The two commonly used methods of providing for depreciation in practice are:

1 straight line;
2 reducing balance.

The first involves the estimation of the life of the asset and the allocation of its cost, in equal instalments, over that life.

The second method requires the application of the same proportion of the balance (book value) at the beginning of each period to be charged as the measure of the cost of use in that accounting period. The proportion to be applied can be calculated by reference to the following formula:

$$1 - \sqrt[N]{(S/C)}$$

where: N = number of years
         S = scrap value
         C = cost of asset

The examples shown in Tables 3.8 and 3.9 will illustrate the application of the two methods. An asset costs £120,000 and is estimated to have a life of ten years, with an estimated residual value of £13,000.

Table 3.8 Straight-line depreciation

Year		£
0	Cost	120,000
1	Depreciation	10,700
	Book value	109,300
2	Depreciation	10,700
	Book value	98,600
3	Depreciation	10,700
	Book value	87,900
⋮		⋮
9	Depreciation	10,700
	Book value	23,700
10	Depreciation	10,700
	Book value	13,000

Table 3.9 Reducing balance depreciation

Year		£
0	Cost	120,000
1	Depreciation (20% × £120,000)	24,000
	Book value	96,000
2	Depreciation (20% × £96,000)	19,200
	Book value	76,800
3	Depreciation (20% × £76,800)	15,400
	Book value	61,400
9	Depreciation (20% × £20,100)	4,000
	Book value	16,100
10	Depreciation (20% × £16,100)	3,200
	Book value	12,900

It will immediately be apparent that the choice of depreciation technique will affect the reported profit figures, not over the ten-year life, but for every discrete period within that time-span. The use of the straight-line method charges the same amount in each time period, whereas the use of the reducing balance method results in higher charges in the earlier periods and lower amounts in the later periods. Advocates of the latter method claim that it reflects the reality of depreciation, but it is common practice, in the United Kingdom, to use the straight-line method for most items of plant and equipment.

One further aspect of depreciation that requires explanation is the accounting treatment arising on the sale of an asset before its useful life has expired. Two situations can arise, first where the asset is sold at a value above that in the records, and second where the sale value is below the book value. The variances of the sale value from the book value would be recorded in the profit statement either as 'profit on sale of asset' or as 'loss on sale of asset'. Clearly, in neither case has a profit or loss been incurred – all that has happened is that the provision for depreciation has been either too generous or inadequate, and once the market value has been ascertained (by a sale) then an adjustment to the previous estimates is made in the year of sale.

ILLUSTRATION

The preparation of a balance sheet illustrating both the underlying cash transactions and the application of accounting conventions can be made by utilising the data contained in the illustration in Chapter 2.

Table 3.10 Calculation of creditors

Due to suppliers	600
Accrued loan interest	100
Taxation per P & L account	280
Dividends per P & L account	415
	1,395

Table 3.11 Balance sheet

Balance sheet as at 30 June 19X9	£000
Fixed assets at cost	10,900
Less depreciation	5,010
	5,890
Current assets	
Stocks	1,500
Debtors	2,000
Cash	400
	3,900
Less current liabilities	
Creditors due within one year	1,395
Net current assets	2,505
Total assets less current liabilities	7,515
Less creditors due after one year:	
Loan capital	1,800
Total net assets	5,715
Financed by:	
Issued ordinary share capital	4,000
Reserves	1,715
	5,715

The detail of the fixed assets has already been calculated and the information for stocks and debtors has been noted. The cash balance will be the opening balance as adjusted by the transactions listed. 'Creditors due within one year' requires summarising as shown in Table 3.10. Finally the 'Reserves' require increasing by this year's retained profits, to £1,715,000.

CONCLUSION

Notwithstanding the implications regarding the subjective choice that is available to the preparers of accounts, it should be realised that the balance sheet is a very important document – it has been described as 'the window to the firm'. Provided that the subjective elements are borne in mind, a great deal of useful information can be obtained from a sensible analysis of the document and by a comparison of any one balance sheet with those immediately preceding it.

KEY LEARNING POINTS

- **The balance sheet shows the assets and liabilities of the business.**
- **The balance sheet shows the sources of the capital employed by the business.**
- **The most important entry is the amount of capital employed, or total assets less current liabilities.**
- **The secondary values are:**
  - **fixed assets;**
  - **working capital;**
  - **loan capital;**
  - **shareholders' funds.**
- **It is dynamic and constantly reflects the values of the transactions of the business.**
- **The values are recorded at their historic cost and do not reflect market (realisable) values.**
- **Fixed assets are recorded at cost less depreciation.**
- **Any change in the value of the assets is reflected in the shareholders' funds, either as a profit (or loss) from trading transactions, or as a gain (or loss) from asset revaluation.**

CASE STUDY

Preparation of balance sheet

Prepare a Balance sheet for Peter French at 31 December 19X2 in the same format as that shown in Table 3.3. The depreciation charge for the year has already been calculated (Chapter 2), but it is necessary to show the depreciation to date in the balance sheet, and these figures need to be added to those shown at 31 December 19X1 (as shown in Table 3.12). The motor vehicle was sold at its net book value, so no further adjustment is necessary in respect of the vehicle sold.

It is necessary to calculate the prepayments in respect of both rent and rates and insurances, and to calculate the creditors and reserves for material suppliers, wages, heating and lighting and telephone, and for accountancy charges. The details necessary for these calculations are shown in Table 3.13.

It is possible to calculate the cash balance at 31 December from the recorded transactions, but for the purpose of the preparation it is an overdraft of £3,600.

Further consideration

Consider the main points of the chapter, summarised above, and identify the significant entries in the balance sheet.

Although the balance sheet is an accounting statement that records the book (historic cost) value of uncompleted transactions at a particular date, it is very often used as a basis for determining the value of a business. Consider the balance sheet that you have prepared and reflect on the extent to which it represents the value of the business to the shareholders. What is the 'balance sheet' value per £1 ordinary share? If you were a shareholder, do you think that this would represent a 'fair' value? How would you value a shareholding, and what criteria would you apply?

Table 3.12 Balance sheets for 19X0 and 19X1

Balance sheet as at 31 December	£000	
	19X0	*19X1*
Fixed assets		
Tangible assets	15.9	15.2
Goodwill	50.0	50.0
Total fixed assets	65.9	65.2
Current assets		
Stocks	12.0	13.6
Debtors	3.8	4.0
Cash and Bank	−2.5	7.7
Total current assets	13.3	25.3
Less current liabilities		
Trade creditors and accruals	14.5	14.9
Taxation	2.7	4.7
Total current liabilities	17.2	19.6
Net current assets	−3.9	5.7
Total assets less current liabilities	62.0	70.9
Less loan	45.0	40.0
Total net assets	17.0	30.9
Financed by:		
Issued ordinary share capital	1.0	1.0
Reserves	16.0	29.9
Shareholders' funds	17.0	30.9
Tangible assets:		
Car (cost)	8.0	8.0
Car (book value)	6.0	4.5
Plant (cost)	16.0	18.0
Plant (book value)	9.9	10.7

Table 3.13 Detailed transactions for 19X0 and 19X1

Details of the various entries for the two years are:		£000	
		19X0	*19X1*
Sales			
Repair		103.4	117.5
Contract		60.0	45.0
Manufactured goods		68.9	76.5
Other goods		35.0	40.0
Carpets		20.0	25.0
Curtains		8.0	10.0
Totals		295.3	314.0
Materials used			
Repair		30.1	33.8
Contract		48.0	36.0
Manufactured goods		24.5	27.6
Other goods		23.7	27.1
Carpets		10.0	12.5
Curtains		4.0	5.0
Totals		140.3	142.0
Salaries			
Office		7.0	7.5
Shop		18.0	18.9
Cleaner		3.0	3.2
Totals		28.0	29.6
Other overheads			
Rent & rates	– unit	5.3	5.4
	– storage	1.2	1.2
	– shop	3.5	4.0
Heating & lighting	– unit	0.9	1.0
	– shop	0.7	0.8
Telephone	– unit	0.8	1.0
	– shop	0.3	0.4
Insurance		2.5	2.7
Car expenses		1.5	1.6
Van expenses		1.9	2.3
Van lease		2.4	2.4
Accountancy etc.		1.5	1.5
Other		1.2	1.3
Depreciation	– car	2.0	1.5
	– plant	1.1	1.2
Totals		26.8	28.3

Chapter 4

Cash flow reports

INTRODUCTION

Since March 1992, all companies have been required to produce a cash flow report, in addition to the other financial reports comprising the balance sheet and profit and loss account. This report replaced the statement of source and application of funds which had been a requirement, in accordance with SSAP 10, since January 1976.

Cash flow reports are significantly different from funds flow reports, in that they identify inflows and outflows of cash and report on the effect of these cash transactions on the firm's cash resources – they identify and draw attention to the change that has taken place in the firm's cash balances. Although this information is available in the balance sheet, in that it can be obtained from the net current assets summary, and any change can be obtained by comparison with the same figures for the previous year, the underlying flows are not reported, nor is attention drawn to these flows, in either of the other two reports. Funds flow reports were designed to identify how a firm has financed its activities during a particular period, and to draw attention to any underlying changes in its working capital (net current asset) position.

The importance of cash flow reports cannot be overemphasised and it is crucial that the benefits of this report are fully understood by readers of annual reports and accounts.

The primary purpose of any business enterprise is to maximise the shareholders' (owners') wealth, and the most pertinent measure of that wealth is in cash.

Assets that are reported in the balance sheet are valued at historic (original) cost; in the case of some fixed assets this amount is reduced by a depreciation charge. The values shown are not realisable values and the balance sheet value of the issued shares (i.e. the total net assets divided by the number of ordinary shares) is not intended to be a measure of the value of those shares. Because the values are recorded at historic cost and because of the presence of price inflation the market (i.e. realisable) value of the assets may be markedly different from that reported in the balance sheet, even after the assets have been depreciated.

There have been two attempts in the United Kingdom since 1973 to prepare balance sheets showing the effects of price inflation. However, because of the complexity of the necessary adjustments, and also because of the highly subjective nature of the approaches, neither attempt was successful, in that these reports generally were ignored for the purposes of interpreting firm's financial positions or progress.

Although the introduction of funds flow statements was a step in the right direction, in terms of drawing attention to the underlying implications (in respect of funds flow) of a firm's trading activities, the main criticism of these reports was that they were prepared under the same conventions as the other reports. It was specifically stated in SSAP 10 that the purpose of the statement was 'to make explicit that which was implicit' in the balance sheet and profit and loss account. Funds flow statements most certainly achieved this objective, but the fact that they were derived from the other financial reports was an inherent weakness and detracted from their usefulness, because these reports are prepared under the accounting conventions, with their judgemental bias, and because the funds flow statement did not specifically emphasise the singular importance of cash.

Cash flow reports are not prepared under accounting conventions, indeed they intentionally ignore such practices, and they specifically report movements of cash.

It is worth remembering: profit is opinion, but cash is fact.

THE CASH FLOW REPORT

David Tweedie, chairman of the Accounting Standards Board, commented: 'You can't fiddle cash flow reports. . . . Cash is the life blood of a business, if it dwindles the business will die. But it is also a very difficult figure to fiddle.' In September 1991 the board issued Financial Reporting Standard No. 1 (FRS 1), *Cash Flow Statements*, which became applicable to all financial statements relating to accounting periods ending after 23 March 1992. This statement replaced the 'statement of source and application of funds' (SSAP 10). This statement, introduced in 1975, is of relatively recent origin. What, then, are cash flow statements, how do they differ from funds flow statements, and what advantages are perceived for the proposed reports?

The academic justification for such reports is that they are objective and free from bias. They are free from the bias arising from the use of subjective judgement utilised in the preparation of the profit statement and balance sheet. The use of subjective judgement is necessary because of the need to apply the accounting conventions.

A cash flow report is, quite simply, a summarised statement of all receipts and payments, suitably analysed, for an accounting period. The report identifies those elements of cash flow, both receipts and payments, suitably classified between the economic, operating, investing and financing activities which together make up the net movement of cash in any given period. It will succinctly identify both the amount and source of cash flowing into a firm and the disbursement of those inflows, also identifying the consequent change in cash position during the period under review. It will make immediately apparent the extent to which different sources of receipts of cash have been utilised to finance the operations of the business.

A funds flow statement is based largely on the differences between the balance sheets at the start and end of a financial period and, while it reorganises such information, it does not of itself produce any new information. As emphasised in SSAP 10, the funds flow statement merely makes explicit that which is implicit in the conventional financial reports. Funds flow statements are dependent on the subjective judgements used to produce those reports and are therefore subject to the bias of the preparer. Although they identify the funds generated from trading activities, by disregarding provisions for depreciation of fixed assets and by disregarding provisions for taxation and dividend distribution, the key element of change to the working capital position is highly dependent on the accounting bases of valuation and indefinite life. A specific criticism of these statements is that there is no emphasis of the impact on the cash resources of the transactions summarised.

Cash flow reports on the other hand are completely objective, in that no allowance is made for stockholding or for credit given to customers or taken from suppliers. They will therefore crucially identify the extent to which the trading activities of a business are dependent on the cash generated from current operations. Additionally the sources of finance for the investment policies of the firm will be highlighted, as will the extent to which these are dependent on external sources of funds.

A more significant justification for cash flow reports is the universal importance of cash to a firm. The primary function of firms is to maximise shareholder wealth over time, and this is measured most objectively in cash terms.

PRESENTATION

FRS 1 allows for the presentation of cash flow reports by either the direct or indirect methods. A direct cash flow report would be one that had been prepared from the accounting records of the firm either by recording the gross receipts and payments or by adjusting sales, cost of sales and other items in the profit and loss account for non-cash items, and changes in working capital and other items which relate to financing or investing activities.

The indirect method commences with the operating profit and shows those adjustments necessary for non-cash items such as depreciation, changes in working capital and financing and investing activities. The preferred layouts for such statements will evolve with time, according to the custom and practice of major concerns, and will undoubtedly be the subject of further regulation as time passes.

In the short term, the student and the analyst will be confined to consideration of reports produced by the indirect method and derived from the conventional financial reports. The exposure draft gives examples of the presentation of statements by both methods. In each case the statement is broadly analysed into the cash flows from operating activities, financing and investing activities.

Table 4.1 is an illustration of a cash flow report produced by the indirect method. The report succinctly identifies the dilemma arising from the nature of profit and of the necessary, but ancillary, need to fund business activity by cash resources. The profit statement shows some £214,000 earned for the year, which the cash flow report reduces to £188,000 as 'cash flow arising from trading activities', that is, the amount of cash 'earned' by the sales in the year, and then reveals that other necessary financing activities involving cash have further reduced this figure to a negative outflow of cash for the year of £235,000. This is due to the payment of interest (on loan capital), dividends and the purchase of additional fixed assets, less a very small increase in both loan capital and issued share capital. All of this information is contained in the other financial reports, profit statement and balance sheet, but because of the manner in which the information is presented these do not make such detail readily apparent.

After deduction of the costs of servicing capital (both loan and equity) and for taxation, the funds available for investment (or return of capital) are revealed. After the deduction for the necessary investment in refurbishment, maintenance and expansion of fixed assets, any additional sources of capital (or redemptions) are recorded and the impact on the current cash position revealed.

The cash flow report identifies the cash generated by operating activities. It itemises the cost of servicing the capital of the firm, to identify the net cash generated in the accounting period. It then reveals both the extent

Table 4.1 Cash flow report

Cash flow report for the year ended 31 December

	£000
Profit per accounts	214
Add depreciation	38
Increase in stocks	(235)
Increase in debtors	(81)
Increase in creditors	252
Net cash flow from operating activities	188
Servicing of finance:	
Interest paid	(15)
Dividends paid	(59)
	114
Taxation paid	(112)
	2
Investing activities:	
purchase of fixed assets (net)	(282)
Net cash inflow before financing	(280)
Financing:	
Increase in loan capital	15
Increase in share capital	30
Increase (decrease) in cash and cash equivalents	(235)

and source of any further capital that has been introduced. Any investment that has been made in the assets of the firm is then deducted.

Thus the cash flow report will crucially reveal the extent to which future investment is being funded by borrowings or increases in equity capital – neither of which is particularly clear from conventional financial reports.

ILLUSTRATION

The data contained in the illustration used to demonstrate the preparation of a profit statement and a balance sheet in the preceding chapters can now be utilised to illustrate the principles of the preparation of cash flow reports. Although the former reports reveal the profit made in the year, and the state of assets and liabilities at the end of the year, it is difficult to identify the source and disposition of cash. It will be noted that the balance for loan capital is £1,800,000 but this figure conceals the fact that a further £1,000,000 has been raised and £200,000 repaid.

Table 4.2 Cash flow report

Cash flow report for the year ended 30 June 19X9	£000	£000
Operating profit		1,310
Add depreciation		1,090
Less increase in working capital		(1,300)
Net flow from operating activities		1,100
Less servicing of capital:		
Interest paid	100	
Dividends paid	100	200
		900
Less taxation paid		600
		300
Investing activities:		
Purchase of fixed assets		900
Net cash inflow before financing		(600)
Financing:		
Additional loan capital (net)		800
Increase in cash		200

The figures have been derived as follows:

- The operating profit and depreciation have been taken from the profit and loss account.
- The incease in working capital has been calculated as follows:

	£000	
	19X8	*19X9*
Debtors	1,000	2,000
Stocks	1,000	1,500
Creditors	(400)	(600)
	1,600	2,900
Increase		+1,300

- The interest paid, dividends paid and purchase of fixed assets have all been obtained from the summary of financial transactions in the introduction to the illustration in Chapter 2.
- The 'taxation paid' is the figure shown in the opening balance sheet and must have been paid as the creditor for taxation shown above is the charge for the year as shown in the profit and loss account.

- As previously explained, the increase in loan capital is the net figure of the additional loan, less the annual repayment.

Again, the utility of the cash flow report is demonstrated, in that information which is not specifically identified in the other financial reports is highlighted in the process of identifying the cash generated from operating activities and how that cash has been used.

CONCLUSIONS

There has been great concern and much debate over the past two decades about the impact of inflation on published reports and it is suggested that cash flow reports present a potential solution to this problem. All that is required is that each year's report is indexed by the use of a suitable rate reflecting the impact of inflation, either generally or specifically as it affects an individual firm, to achieve the presentation of reports for both the current cost and the adjusted cost. A significant amount of consideration will need to be given to such a proposition, but it is submitted that such an approach would at least have the merit of being understandable, which is more than can be claimed for the current cost accounting approach. This was an attempt to adjust financial reports to reflect the impact of changing prices, but was abandoned because of its complexity.

Thus the cash flow report adds a particularly valuable source of information to the interested user of accounts, in that all pretensions that might be invoked by the use of 'cosmetic' accounting procedures are dispensed with and, as Mr Tweedie has observed, the facts are laid bare. It confirms the fundamental truth that 'profit is opinion whereas cash is fact'.

KEY LEARNING POINTS

- **The cash flow report emphasises the singular importance of cash to a business.**
- **The preparation of the report ignores the conventions used in the preparation of the other financial reports.**
- **The report highlights the various sources of cash during the period, detailing how and where these have been invested in the business.**

CASE STUDY

Preparation of cash flow reports

Prepare a cash flow report for Peter French for the year ending 31 December 19X3 from the balance sheet prepared after Chapter 3 and that shown for 19X2.

Comparison with the other financial reports

Consider the differences between the information revealed by the cash flow report and that revealed by the other financial reports, and identify the unique claims that have been made for the cash flow report.

Chapter 5

Accounting for inflation

In Chapter 4 it was suggested that cash flow reports, suitably adjusted by some form of price index, could offer a solution to the perennial problem of accounting for the impact of changing prices – inflation.

THE NATURE OF THE PROBLEM

The root of this problem lies in the accounting convention of historical cost. This requires that all transactions are recorded in the financial reports at their acquisition cost. The result of this is a balance sheet which reports investments that have been made over a number of years at differing cost prices. An analogy can be made that the total of a balance sheet is merely the total of 'different types of fruit', e.g. apples, pears and plums, making no distinction between either the numbers of these different fruits or their relative values. In the profit and loss account the depreciation charge in any one year comprises a proportion of each of the different 'fruits' – i.e. the use of the asset, which may all have been used to produce the same output, is charged at different rates reflecting the cost of the asset. Thus the resultant profit is overstated by the extent of the understatement of depreciation. Additionally, where goods have been purchased for resale, and their cost rises prior to that sale taking place, the resultant profit is overstated in real terms by the increase due to the rise in the cost price.

The justification for the application of the historical cost convention is that the resultant reports are objective, in that the values utilised are verifiable. Further problems arise with the application of both the realisation and conservatism conventions, however. The former requires that profit is only recorded when a transaction takes place, while the latter requires that only estimates of losses are included in the reports, and that any future profit is ignored, thus ensuring that reported profits are distributable – i.e. that they have been received. There is an exception to this rule (previously mentioned), in that estimates of increases in the value of land and buildings are recorded in the balance sheet in order to report the current market value of the asset.

The consequence of the application of these conventions is that, during periods of rising prices, the 'real' values of the shareholders' funds are understated and the amount of profit reported in the profit and loss account is overstated.

THE FUNCTION OF FINANCIAL REPORTS

This outcome leads to a much more fundamental question as to the function and purpose of financial reports. The function of the balance sheet is to measure the value of the business as represented by the shareholders' funds, and the function of the profit statement is to measure the income (profit) of the enterprise, produced by the employment of that capital, during the period under review. Such a discussion is beyond the scope of this book, but an indication of the nature of the dilemma can be given by considering the analogy of an orchard. The capital is represented by the trees in the orchard, which produce the fruit which can be sold – the income. The problem is the method of valuation to be applied to the orchard.

- Is it to be valued at historical cost – the cost of planting the trees?
- Is the cost of maintaining and nurturing the trees to be treated as a deduction from the income arising from selling the fruit?
- Or is the orchard to be valued at its market value (the net proceeds of selling it)?
- Or at the cost of replacing the orchard?
- Or further, is the historical cost to be recorded after adjustment for the effects of inflation?

Another valuation concept that could be utilised is that of present value, which is an economic concept under which the orchard would be valued at the discounted value of the estimates of the future benefits arising from its continued use. Although there is very great practical merit in this approach, which is often used intuitively for valuation purposes in practice, it is undoubtedly an approach where nearly all, if not all, the variables used for the valuation are derived subjectively.

THE CONCEPT OF 'REAL' VALUES

Another aspect of the problem of changing prices arises in the determination of how much of the reported profit is distributable, or consumable. In other words, how much of the after-tax profits of an enterprise can be distributed as dividends without reducing, in 'real terms', the value of the enterprise. Paradoxically, the purpose of the application of the prudence convention is to ensure that subscribed capital is not distributed as dividend. However, the effect of not allowing for the impact of changing prices could, and probably would, lead to this very situation.

Consider an analogy with a deposit in a savings account of £10,000 earning an after-tax rate of interest of 8 per cent. If inflation is 4 per cent, how much of the interest can be withdrawn for consumption, and how much must be left in the account to maintain its purchasing power in real terms? Clearly, half the interest represents the impact of inflation, and the account should be increased by this amount to retain its value in real terms. However, if no account is taken of inflation when calculating the profit earned during a year, then the distribution of dividends may result in the real value of the shareholders' capital being reduced.

PROBLEMS OF HISTORIC COST ACCOUNTING

The effects of the application of the accounting conventions during periods of inflation can be explained in the following manner.

Cost convention

A firm buys machinery costing £10,000 with which it produces and sells goods. Some time later it buys another item of machinery, exactly the same as the first, in order to double its output. The second machine costs £20,000. Under the cost convention the assets are recorded at £30,000 (before depreciation), but the second machine is neither twice as large as the first, nor will it produce twice the output. It will produce the same amount of output, but in calculating the profit earned from both machines the charge for use (depreciation) of the second machine is double the amount for the first.

Clearly, any measurement of the profit as a return on the capital employed (see Chapter 7) will be distorted as a result of inflation.

Realisation convention

The effect of the application of this convention is that profit is only recorded when a transaction takes place, and that any increases in value during the period in which the asset is held are ignored. (The exception to this principle is the case of land and buildings.) For example, if goods purchased at £100 for resale are sold immediately, realising £120, that would give rise to a profit of £20. If, however, they are held in stock for some time, during which the cost rises to £200, and are then sold for £240, a profit is recorded of £140. Part of this profit is a gain due to holding the stock during periods of price change, and is needed to maintain the value of the capital employed in real terms. In other words, it should not be distributed as dividend because it will be needed to purchase the replacement goods, the cost of which has now risen to £200. Thus the position in real terms is that a profit of £40 has been earned and a holding gain of £100 has accrued.

The nature of the problems outlined can be summarised as follows:

- How should the assets and liabilities be valued in the balance sheet?
- How should profit be calculated so as to ensure that the distribution of dividends does not reduce the real value of the shareholders' capital?

INFLATION ACCOUNTING TECHNIQUES

A number of different methods of valuation are available, all of which have advantages and disadvantages, and some of which have been applied unsuccessfully in the recent past. These methods are examined below.

Current purchasing power

Under this approach, adjustments are made to the historical cost accounts by means of the application of a price index, such as the retail price index. An attempt was made in 1974 to introduce this method into the United Kingdom (SSAP 7) by the utilisation of the retail price index, but it was generally poorly received and was withdrawn in 1978.

The method distinguishes between, on the one hand, monetary assets and liabilities under which the holders of these – debtors, cash, loans, etc. – suffer losses due to the impact of inflation over time, and on the other hand, liabilities, creditors and overdrafts where inflation produces gains in real terms over time. This is because receipts from, say, debtors, or payments to creditors are reduced, in real terms, by the time the transaction is completed. Alternatively, settlements in the future of liabilities are a benefit because these also are made in a 'depreciated' currency. The other category is of non-monetary items, such as fixed assets, stocks and shareholders' funds.

In the profit and loss account the effect is to adjust for holding gains, that is the benefit of the increase in the cost of goods for resale due to inflation, so that the reported profit is reduced to that earned in real terms. In the balance sheet the non-monetary items are adjusted to reflect the increase in the price index and the resulting gain is shown as part of the shareholders' funds.

It should be appreciated that it is not the intention of this approach that the financial reports should reflect market values.

Current value accounting

There are a number of approaches that can reflect current values:

- replacement cost accounting;
- realisable value accounting;
- current cost accounting.

Replacement cost accounting

Under this approach the deduction of costs and expenses in the profit and loss account is recorded using current replacement costs, not the historical costs incurred, thus reporting profit in real terms. The difference between this calculation and the traditional historic cost calculation is shown as a holding gain, that is the benefit that has arisen through holding goods for resale, over time, during periods of price increases.

In the balance sheet, assets are shown at their replacement cost. The difference between this and their historic cost is shown as a revaluation reserve, as part of the shareholders' funds. It should be stressed that assets that are some years old are shown at their current replacement cost less the appropriate depreciation, on that cost, to reflect their age.

Realisable value accounting

This is a similar approach to replacement cost accounting, but one where realisable values, net of selling costs, are utilised instead of replacement costs. It is a much more conservative approach and may result in losses being recorded due to the fact that a business is, in effect, being valued at its break-up value, rather than as a going concern.

Current cost accounting

This is a hybrid approach that utilises elements of both of the above methods of current value accounting. It was introduced into the United Kingdom in 1980 (SSAP 16) but was generally regarded as too technical and was to all intents and purposes ignored by both readers and analysts of accounts. It was withdrawn in 1984. Perhaps the most significant factor in its unpopularity, and ultimate demise, was that the Inland Revenue refused to countenance its use for taxation purposes.

ILLUSTRATION

The historic cost accounts shown in Table 5.1 can be used as a simplified illustration of the above methods. It should be stressed that the illustration is very much simplified, in order to establish the principle of both the effect of changing prices and of the methods themselves.

Table 5.1 Historic cost accounts

Profit and loss account for the year ended 31 December 19X1

		£000
Sales		200
Cost of sales		120

Gross profit		80
Overhead expenses	25	
Depreciation	10	35
	---	---
Operating profit		45

Balance sheet as at 31 December 19X1

		£000
Fixed assets		100
Depreciation		10

		90
Stocks	30	
Debtors	20	
Cash	10	

	60	
Less creditors	10	

Net current assets		50

Total assets less current liabilities		140
Loan		20

Total net assets		120

Financed by:		
Issued ordinary shares		50
Profit and loss account		70

		120

Current purchasing power accounting

Consider a situation where a retail price index was 100 at the commencement of the year and had risen to 120 at the end of the year. The accounts shown in Table 5.2 would be prepared utilising the current purchasing power approach.

Table 5.2 CPP accounts

Profit and loss account for the year ended 31 December 19X1

	HC accounts £000	Conversion factor	CPP accounts £000
Sales	200	120/110	218
Cost of sales	120	120/110	131
Gross profit	80		87
Overhead expenses	25	120/110	27
Depreciation	10	120/100	12
Operating profit	45		48
Less price gain			5
Profit			43

Balance sheet as at 31 December 19X1

	HC accounts £000	Conversion factor	CPP accounts £000
Fixed assets	100	120/100	120
Depreciation	10	120/100	12
	90		108
Stocks	30	120/110	33
Debtors	20	120/120	20
Cash	10	120/120	10
	150		171
Less creditors	10	120/120	10
	140		161
Less loan	20	100/120	17
Total net assets	120		144
Financed by:			
Issued ordinary shares	50	120/120	50
Share capital maintenance reserve			10
Profit and loss account	70		68
Purchasing power gain			16
	120		144

The adjustments that have been made are at the average of the increase over the year, with the exception of that for depreciation which has been adjusted to show the impact of the year's change.

Table 5.3 Calculation of purchasing power gain

	£000
Increase in value of:	
fixed assets	20
stocks	3
loan (reduced purchasing power)	3
Less share capital maintenance	(10)
	16

It should be pointed out that the profit and loss account figure in the CPP balance sheet is erroneous and that an adjustment would have been made in the previous year, which is not shown in this illustration. The calculation of the purchasing power gain is made as shown in Table 5.3. Thus the CPP accounts reveal the impact of inflation, in that the real value of the profit is reduced showing how much can be distributed as dividends and how much (of the HC profits) must be retained in order to maintain, in real terms, the value of the capital employed. It should be noted that the CPP value of the loan reduces because this will be repaid in the future in a 'depreciated' currency.

Replacement cost accounting

The same example can be used to illustrate the preparation of replacement cost accounts (see Table 5.4). The following are the relevant replacement costs:

	£000
Fixed assets (one year old)	120
Stock	36
Cost of sales	130

The effect of the adjustments is to show how much of the profit can be distributed and to value the impact of changing prices on both the assets and the capital employed in the balance sheet. Table 5.5 details the revaluation reserve. The latter figure is the increase in value of both the fixed assets and the stock at their replacement cost.

Realisable value accounting

For technical reasons it is not possible to use the same example to illustrate the application of net realisable value accounting, because it would be necessary to produce a set of realisable values in respect of the assets at the commencement of the year.

The method is very similar to that shown in the previous illustration, except that instead of using replacement cost it utilises realisable value. For example, consider the case of an asset purchased for £100,000 which has a net realisable value of £150,000 at the end of the year. During the next year the realisable value rises to £180,000 and the asset is sold for £250,000 during the third year. The gains are reported as shown in Table 5.6. The total gain is £150,000, which would have been shown in year three under the historic cost convention, whereas this method apportions the gain over the three years of ownership.

Current cost accounting

The current cost accounting approach is highly technical and extremely complex; for this reason no attempt has been made to illustrate this method.

CONCLUSIONS

Both the mechanics of, and rationale for, inflation accounting are confusing. It will be understood that this has been a contentious issue for very many years. There is no consensus, in the accounting profession, on either the approach to adopt, or the necessity for any adjustment to the traditional historic cost accounts. It cannot be disputed that the great strength of this approach is the fact that it is objective and that the values used are capable of verification.

Equally, there can be no doubt that the impact of inflation does distort financial reports and that, over time, it makes them misleading. It cannot be argued that 'low' rates of inflation make the necessity for adjustment redundant. Consider the effect of such 'low' rates of inflation as shown in Table 5.7 makes a succint point about the nature of inflation. At a 'low' rate of inflation of 1 per cent, the value of assets is reduced by 10 per cent in ten years. At the higher rate of 5 per cent they are decimated to only 60 per cent of their value over the same period. Even a rate of 3 per cent reduces the value of assets by a quarter in that period. The reader will no doubt appreciate why the view is held, and has been for a very long time, that investments in property are inflation-proof. This view will hold good despite the crisis experienced in the property market during the early 1990s.

Table 5.4 Replacement cost accounts

Profit and loss account for the year ended 31 December 19X1

	HC accounts £000	RC accounts £000
Sales	200	200
Cost of sales	120	130
Gross profit	80	70
Overhead expenses	25	25
Depreciation	10	12
Operating profit	45	33

Balance sheet as at 31 December 19X1	*£000*	*£000*
Fixed assets	100	120
Depreciation	10	12
	90	108
Stocks	30	36
Debtors	20	20
Cash	10	10
	150	174
Less creditors	10	10
	140	164
Loan	20	20
Total net assets	120	144
Financed by:		
Issued ordinary shares	50	50
Profit and loss account	70	58
Revaluation reserve		36
	120	144

In Chapter 7, which deals with the analysis and interpretation of financial reports, it is recommended that five years of reports are necessary in order to make an efficient appraisal of company performance. It can be seen from the above table that significant adjustments will be necessary to such figures, in order to make a meaningful comparison over a five-year period even when there have been only 'low' rates of inflation.

Table 5.5 Calculation of revaluation reserve

	£000
Realised holding gain (P & L account)	12
Unrealised holding gain (balance sheet)	24
	36

Table 5.6 Realisable value accounting

		£000
Year 1	Unrealised gain (150–100)	£50
Year 2	Unrealised gain (180–150)	30
Year 3	Realised gain (250–180)	70
	Total gain	150

Table 5.7 Effects of 'low' rates of inflation

Rate of inflation	1.0%	2.0%	3.0%	4.0%	5.0%
Year 1	0.99	0.98	0.97	0.96	0.95
Year 2	0.98	0.96	0.94	0.92	0.90
Year 3	0.97	0.94	0.91	0.88	0.86
Year 4	0.96	0.92	0.89	0.85	0.81
Year 5	0.95	0.90	0.86	0.82	0.77
Year 6	0.94	0.88	0.83	0.78	0.74
Year 7	0.93	0.87	0.81	0.75	0.70
Year 8	0.92	0.85	0.78	0.72	0.66
Year 9	0.91	0.83	0.76	0.69	0.63
Year 10	0.90	0.81	0.73	0.66	0.60

**There can be no doubt that there is a compelling case for the
adjustment to financial reports in respect of price changes and that
the only question that remains is concerning the most appropriate
technique. It has previously been suggested that any adjustment to
the cash flow report by means of a suitable price index could be a
solution. Perhaps, in the not too distant future, a further Financial
Reporting Standard will be introduced, requiring the publication of
an additional report which will embody such a statement.**

KEY LEARNING POINTS

- **The strength of the traditional historic cost convention for the preparation of financial reports is its objectivity and capacity for verification.**
- **The problems inherent in such an approach result in the overstatement of distributable profits and the understatement of shareholders' funds, in real terms, during periods of rising prices.**
- **The variety of approaches to the resolution of this problem merely gives rise to confusion as to the purpose and function of financial reports.**
- **One possible solution is to adjust the cash flow report by means of a suitable price index.**
- **The problems inherent in the impact of rising prices are not resolved by the achievement of 'low' rates of inflation – they (the problems) are merely mitigated to some extent.**

CASE STUDY

To what extent would the preparation of inflation adjusted accounts be of any value to Peter French?

Chapter 6

Cash forecasting

INTRODUCTION

The singular importance of cash as an element in the management of a firm's resources has been stressed during the discussion on cash flow reports.

> **It cannot be over-emphasised that more firms fail because of problems of liquidity (cash shortage) than because of lack of profitability. In view of the fact that a large number of firms are taken over (at considerably less than their market value) because of liquidity problems, the importance of cash management becomes paramount.**

Paradoxically, cash management is probably the only area of forecasting that can be undertaken, in the short term, with a great deal of accuracy. Most firms will be able to forecast cash inflows for the ensuing two to three months from the current debtors position and from the current order book. Retail organisations will have different problems, but it is very rare that receipts in the immediate future will vary greatly from current levels or from last year's patterns duly amended for any current trends. Similarly, because the current order book is known, a confident forecast of outgoings can be made in relation to the production requirements for the short-term future. Firms will need to produce forecasts for at least the next financial year; the latter part of this forecast will be more subjective than the earlier months. Notwithstanding these problems, the management of cash in the short term is a crucial requirement, and such an annual forecast can be regularly amended during the year in order to provide the necessary elements for such control.

All firms will, or should, plan for the longer term. Cash forecasts will be an essential part of the plans and will be necessary in order that the firm will be aware of crucial capital-raising requirements implicit in the satisfactory outcome for the plans.

> **The purpose of the cash forecast (or budget) is to ascertain the effect that the planned levels of output, and their associated costs, will have on the firm's cash resources. The fact that a firm is planning to make a profit in the ensuing year does not automatically**

mean that such profits will result in a cash surplus. In the case of smaller firms that are expanding, it is almost axiomatic that the reverse situation will apply. This arises as a result of what is called the 'trading cycle', which has to be funded.

The trading cycle arises as a result of the need to purchase raw materials and incur expenses, in the form of wages, salaries and other overhead costs, in order to convert the raw materials into finished goods, to hold finished goods in stock, and then to provide for customers' credit. Against the total of this investment is offset any credit that is received from suppliers. Where a firm is undergoing a period of expansion, then the replenishment of stock levels will be at a higher level than the sales that are taking place, thus giving rise to the need for investment of further capital. The profit arising from current levels of activity will almost certainly be inadequate for this purpose.

Such expansion, as experienced by smaller firms, results in what is known as 'over-trading'. This is a situation where payments exceed receipts because of the previously explained need to finance higher levels of stocks, work in progress and debtors, due to the expansion of output. Overtrading is not an unhealthy situation, arising as it does as a direct result of expansion, but it does need to be monitored closely and adequate provision made for the introduction of permanent capital to fund the level of expansion.

The trading cycle can be calculated as shown in Table 6.1. The calculation of the number of days involved in any of the elements is an average and will be made in relation to the annual measure of that element. For example, if raw material stocks are £50,000 and annual purchases are £500,000, and there are 240 working days in the year, then raw material stockholding represents ten working days. Similarly if annual sales are £1,000,000 and customer credit is £200,000, then investment in credit is forty-eight working days. As the annual values change, then so will the amount of the investment relative to the number of days in the trading cycle, and so may the number of days in the trading cycle, if the change between two variables, say sales and debtors, is not at the same rate.

It follows that, in order to maximise the utilisation of cash, investment in all of the elements involved in the trading cycle must be at optimal levels.

Table 6.1 The trading cycle

Raw material stockholding	X days
Work-in-progress	X days
Finished goods stock	X days
Customer credit	X days
	X days
Less credit from suppliers	X days
Trading cycle	X days

That is, that the investment in stocks and debtors should be at the most efficient levels and should not contain any element of either overstocking or excess credit.

Table 6.2 Pro-forma cash budget

Cash budget for the six months to 30 June 19X0

	Jan.	Feb.	Mar.	Apr.	May	Jun.
Receipts						
Sales						
Other receipts	——	——	——	——	——	——
Total receipts	——	——	——	——	——	——
Payments						
Suppliers						
Wages and salaries						
Other expenses						
Other payments	——	——	——	——	——	——
Total payments	——	——	——	——	——	——
Surplus (deficit)						
Balance brought forward						
Balance carried forward						

The principles of the preparation of cash forecasts are relatively straight-forward. Firstly a pro-forma of the generally accepted layout (Table 6.2) is shown, followed by the steps that should be taken for preparation and, finally, the data from which the preparation can be made. The layout will depend on the particular nature of both receipts and payments for a particular firm, and the above reflects the nature of the data in the following illustration.

The principles of preparation are:

1 Enter receipts allowing for customer credit, which must reflect the credit being taken by customers and not the firm's credit policies.
2 Enter any other extraneous receipts in the month that these will be received.
3 Enter payments to suppliers, allowing for both stockholding and the credit actually being taken.
4 Enter payments for the other expenditure in the months that such payments will be made, including any payments in respect of taxation, dividends and the purchase of new assets.
5 Total the receipts for each month.
6 Total the payments for each month.
7 Deduct the payments from the receipts in order to calculate the surplus or deficit for each month.

8 Enter the opening balance as the 'balance brought forward' in the first
month.
9 Add the surplus (or deduct the deficit) to the opening balance (balance
brought forward) in the first month in order to calculate the closing
balance – 'balance carried forward'.
10 This balance then becomes the balance brought forward for the second
month and the process is repeated until the cash forecast is completed.

ILLUSTRATION

The following data relate to the six months to 30 June 19X0.
Budgeted sales are:

January	£100,000	February	£140,000	March	£160,000
April	£180,000	May	£200,000	June	£200,000
July	£200,000				

Customers take two months' credit, which means that receipts from
January's sales will be received in March. There are debtors of £200,000 on
1 January in respect of sales in November and December of £100,000 for
each month.

The goods for resale are purchased two months before the sales are
made and suppliers are paid in the month following receipt of the goods.
The cost of the goods purchased is equal to 40 per cent of the sales value.
The effect of the stockholding means that, for instance, the goods sold in
January of £40,000 (40% × £100,000) were purchased in November and
paid for in December.

Wages and salaries are budgeted as follows, and 25 per cent of the
budgeted figures are deducted as tax and remitted to the Inland Revenue in
the month after deduction. On 1 January £8,000 was owing in respect of
deductions during December.

January	£32,000	February	£32,000	March	£36,000
April	£36,000	May	£40,000	June	£40,000

On 1 April an insurance premium for £10,000 is to be paid; the same
amount was paid in the previous year.

Telephone and electricity accounts in respect of the quarters to 31
December and 31 March are to be paid as follows:

February:	telephone	£10,000,	electricity	£5,000
May:	telephone	£8,000,	electricity	£6,000

The quarter's accounts to 30 June are telephone £10,000 and electricity
£5,000.

Bank interest and charges are budgeted for £3,000 in both March and
June. Other expenses are budgeted as follows:

| January | £30,000 | February | £5,000 | March | £4,000 |
| April | £25,000 | May | £3,000 | June | £30,000 |

Budgeted payments have been made in respect of:

January:	dividends	£30,000
February:	taxation	£20,000
April:	purchase of new plant	£50,000

There are budgeted receipts for February and May for rents received of £10,000 in each month, and receipts of £20,000 in March from the sale of old plant. The cash balance at 1 January is £80,000.

The cash budget can now be prepared in respect of the foregoing data in the pro-forma outlined above as shown in Table 6.3. The function of the cash forecast is pertinently illustrated in that, first, it identifies the effect on the cash resource of the firm's plans for the next period, and second, it identifies particular shortfalls during that period. In this example the firm has substantial deficits during April and May and must take action in order to provide temporary finance to cover these.

The reduction in cash resources is not due to any lack of profitability – on the contrary, the firm is planning for an excellent level of profit, as the budgeted profit statement for the period (Table 6.4) reveals. There is an exceptionally high profit to sales ratio – a wholesaling firm would more usually expect a ratio to be in the order of 5 per cent to 8 per cent. It is an exaggerated illustration, in order to emphasise the importance of cash forecasting – a situation where output doubled in a six-month period would be most unusual. However, it does illustrate the relationship between profit and cash. The reason for the decline in cash resources, despite the very high rate of profit forecast, lies in the increase in value of the 'trading cycle' due to the expansion. The following reconciliation (Table 6.5) between profit and cash highlights the impact of expansion on this investment. The reconciliation in Table 6.3 is of course a form of cash flow report and does therefore enhance the utility of that particular report. It also emphasises the impact of expansion on cash resources and highlights the fact that investment needs to be made prior to the receipt of income from sales.

SOURCES OF SHORT-TERM FINANCE

Where a firm experiences a series of monthly cash deficits due to expansion, it is experiencing the phenomenon of 'over-trading', which merely means that cash receipts are less than cash payments, due to the need to fund investment in working capital for expansion. This is a perfectly normal and natural condition and it is the firm's responsibility to ensure that adequate finance is available. If the expansion envisaged is of a permanent nature then it follows that the finance should also be of a

Table 6.3 Cash budget

Cash budget, six months to 30 June 19X1						
	£000					
	Jan.	*Feb.*	*Mar.*	*Apr.*	*May*	*Jun.*
Receipts						
Sales	100	100	100	140	160	180
Rent		10			10	
Plant			20			
Total receipts	100	110	120	140	170	180
Payments						
Suppliers	56	64	72	80	80	80
Wages etc.,	24	24	27	27	30	30
Inland Revenue	8	8	8	9	9	10
Insurance				10		
Telephone		10			8	
Electricity		5			6	
Bank charges etc.,			3			3
Other expenses	30	5	4	25	3	30
Dividends	30					
Taxation		20				
New plant				50		
Total payments	148	136	114	201	136	153
Surplus (Deficit)	(48)	(26)	6	(61)	34	27
Balance b/forward	80	32	6	12	(49)	(15)
Balance c/forward	32	6	12	(49)	(15)	12

permanent nature, in the form of either share capital or longer-term loans. If the shortages are short-term, then the finance cover can also be of a short-term nature. It should be emphasised that where a firm is considering increasing its capital, of whatever type, it should ensure that working capital – stocks and debtors- are at optimal levels and that there is no excess investment within these areas.

There is a bewildering array of short-term finance facilities available on the financial markets and the following categories are indicative of broad generic types:

- **Bank loans** These are for fixed terms, with regular periodic repayments. The advantage of such a type of provision is that the term is fixed and the advance cannot be called in except for a breach of the conditions attaching to the loan.
- **Bank overdrafts** This is a borrowing facility that provides for temporary deficits up to an agreed limit. Because interest is charged daily on

Table 6.4 Profit and loss account

Profit and loss account for the six months ended 30 June 19X1

		£000
Sales		980
Cost of sales (40%)	392	
Wages	216	608
Gross profit		372
Insurances	10	
Bank charges etc.,	6	
Telephone	18	
Electricity	11	
Other expenses	97	
	142	
Less rents received	20	122
Profit before depreciation		250
Profit to sales ratio		25.5%

Table 6.5 Reconciliation statement

Reconciliation of cash and profit

		£000
Increase in debtors		200
Increase in stocks		64
		264
Less increase in creditors:		
Suppliers	24	
Inland Revenue	2	26
Increase in value of trading cycle		238
Add dividends paid	30	
taxation paid	20	
new plant (net of sales)	30	80
Cash outflow during period		318
Less profit		250
Net outflow		68
Opening cash balance		80
Closing cash balance		12

the outstanding balance, it is a cost effective arrangement. However, because it is a facility and may be agreed to be made available for a specific period, it can be terminated without notice. Overdrafts are therefore unsuitable as a source of finance for anything other than periodic shortages of a fairly temporary nature.

- **Hire purchase and lease purchase**   Both are similar and are appropriate for the purchase of fixed assets. A deposit will be made on purchase and the balance paid, together with interest, over the term of the agreement.
- **Factoring**   This involves an agreement with specialist financial institutions which make advances (usually between 70 per cent to 80 per cent) against debtors. The customer pays the account to the factor, which remits the balance back to his client less interest charges and a small fee based on the face value of the invoice. It is a very appropriate source of finance for the expanding company, in that it provides a finance facility which is geared precisely to the current needs. If sales expand then so does the amount of the facility that is available.
- **Trade creditors**   All too frequently, the first port of call by firms facing cash deficits are their trade creditors and finance is obtained by the simple expedient of not settling accounts on the due date. If a firm does not settle, say, £100,000 of due accounts, but delays payment for a month and then maintains the extended credit it has, in effect, borrowed this amount from its suppliers – without, it should be noted, the tedium of having to present a case or to provide any security. It can be an extremely short-sighted choice, in that, if discounts are lost the annual cost of these can be prohibitively expensive (in terms of the amount raised) and, additionally, the practice may lead to the loss of both supply and credit reputation, which in terms of delivery and prices may turn out to be very expensive.

It should not be assumed that any firm could make use of the complete range of facilities that are available, as some are mutually exclusive. Where advances are obtained from commercial banks, security in the form of a floating debenture on the firm's assets will need to be given. These assets will include debtors, so such an arrangement will probably exclude the possibility of utilising factoring finance, unless the security can be renegotiated. Similarly, hire purchase and lease purchase relate to the acquisition of fixed assets and such assets are then prohibited as security for advances from other sources.

It is necessary that each firm should look at its own individual circumstances and decide on the most appropriate mix of finance for those circumstances at that particular point in time.

CONCLUSIONS

Because of the singular importance of cash to all organisations, both large and small, cash forecasting is arguably the most important management

task in the area of financial planning. The techniques are simple to understand and apply, and because of the essentially short-term nature of the
forecasts, the probability of a high degree of accuracy in these is enhanced.
The early identification of cash shortfalls can assist with planning for the
additional finance, or signal that the rate of expansion is too high for
the current resources of the business. It is unlikely that a profitable, well-
managed firm, of whatever size, will experience great difficulty in obtaining
adequate sources of finance both long and short term.

KEY LEARNING POINTS

- **The singular importance of cash management is emphasised as the crucial element to continued business success.**
- **Variations in the trading cycle are identified as the cause of cash deficits.**
- **The steps in the preparation of cash budgets are clearly itemised and identified.**
- **The common sources of short-term finance have been discussed in this chapter.**

CASE STUDY

Prepare a cash budget for Peter French for the year to 31 December 19X3
on a quarterly basis from the data contained in Table 6.6. Assume that all
quarters have the same number of weeks

All receipts are received in cash and in equal weekly amounts. All
suppliers are paid monthly in arrears. Wages are paid weekly in arrears. In
practice, variations in takings and allowances for holidays would need to be
taken into account. Subcontractors are paid promptly in the month the
liability is incurred. Rates are £2,500 per annum and are paid half-yearly in
May and November. Rents are paid quarterly, commencing on 1 January.
The payment in the fourth quarter is £2,350. Heating, lighting and telephone accounts are paid quarterly in arrears in January, April, July and
October. Insurances are paid in July and accountancy charges in April. All
other expenses are paid monthly as incurred. Taxation in respect of the
previous year's profit is paid in May. The additional plant is purchased and
paid for in April. It can be assumed that all other annual expenses arise
equally on a weekly basis.

All debtors and creditors from the balance sheet at 31 December 19X2
must be taken into account. It should be noted that although creditors for
supplies are paid monthly, this is in respect of purchases. It will be
necessary to determine when the purchases are made so that the stocks are
available as stated in the case study. An example of this type of calculation
is given in Chapter 12.

...ions for 19X3

...are Peter French's budgets for the year to 31 March 19X3:

...stery repair	£131,600
...tracts	50,000
...anufactured products	91,800
Other purchased upholstery	45,000
Carpets	30,000
Curtains etc.	15,000
Total	£363,400

Materials:

Upholstery manufacture	£30,600
Upholstery purchases	38,200
Carpets and curtains	22,500
Other purchases	30,000

Contracts:

Materials etc.	£40,000
Commissions	5,000

Wages:

Craftsmen	£31,200
Assistants	10,400
Retail shop wages	20,000
Cleaner	3,200
Secretary	8,000
Driver and assistant	12,000

Other overheads:

Subcontractors		£17,500
Rent & rates	– unit	5,500
	– storage	1,200
	– retail shop	4,000
Lighting and heating	– unit	1,200
	– shop	1,000
Telephone	– unit	1,200
	– shop	500
Car expenses		1,800
Van expenses		1,500
Interest		6,000
Miscellaneous expenses		1,700
Depreciation	– car	2,800
	– plant	1,600
Lease	– van	2,400
Accountancy & legal fees		2,500
Insurances		3,500
Director's salary		30,000

Capital expenditure:

New plant	£3,000

Chapter 7

Analysis of financial reports

INTRODUCTION

The measure of success in any business is the rate of return earned by that business on the net assets employed. This can be equated to the interest earned on deposit or savings accounts, or to the dividends received from investments in ordinary shares.

The primary purpose of any business is to maximise the return on the investment made by its owners – the ordinary shareholders. The measure that is important to shareholders is that of earnings per share, which is the after-tax profits (earnings) divided by the number of shares that have been issued. This figure is dependent on a number of factors, such as the amount of loan capital incorporated into the capital of the firm and the effective tax rate paid by the firm. Because of this it is first necessary to calculate the return on the capital employed (ROCE) in the business. This is the operating profit (before the deduction of loan interest) expressed as a percentage of the capital employed. This latter figure is the 'total assets less current liabilities' figure in the balance sheet. This comprises the total of both loan capital and the shareholders' funds, which themselves comprise issued share capital and retained profits. This figure is used because it is the amount of capital employed by the management of the firm in investment in assets which have been used to generate the sales which have produced the operating profit. Thus the operating profit, which is calculated before deduction of the cost of loan capital, is the return that has been obtained from the employment of capital. The objectives of the firm should always be towards the maximisation of this measure.

It must be noted that, as with any form of comparative analysis, it is not the value of the ratio itself that is important but its comparison with previous ratios, i.e. the trend. Further, it is not the amount of change in the trend that is important, but the rate of change. A 1 per cent increase from 4 per cent to 5 per cent is a rate of change of 25 per cent, whereas a 1 per cent increase from 25 per cent to 26 per cent is a rate of change of only 4 per cent.

The profit *after* deduction of the loan interest, when measured against the shareholders' funds, provides the measure of return on the shareholders' funds. This will be greater than the ROCE where it (the ROCE) is higher than the cost of loan interest. This provides the recompense to the equity shareholders for the additional risk incurred by introducing debt (loan capital) into the capital employed. The relationship between debt (loan) capital and equity (shareholders') capital is known as 'gearing', and is calculated by expressing the loan capital as a percentage of capital employed (total assets less current liabilities). It can also be calculated by expressing the debt capital as a percentage of the shareholders' funds. When considering the implications of gearing it is always necessary to ascertain the basis on which the calculation has been made.

It should be appreciated that the ROCE does not arise in a random fashion but is the result of the interaction of the amount of capital employed, the sales generated by that capital and the margin earned on those sales.

Table 7.1 Primary ratios

	Year 1 £000	Year 2 £000
Capital	100	120
Sales	200	300
Profit	20	30
ROCE	20%	25%
Margin on sales	10%	10%
Capital (asset) turnover	2.0	2.5

This point can be illustrated by the example shown in Table 7.1. The ROCE has increased to 25 per cent in year 2 because the capital turnover ratio has improved to 2.5. The margin on sales has been maintained at the previous year's level, but the increased efficiency in the management of capital employed has produced additional sales of £0.50 per £ of capital employed, which has earned the margin of 10 per cent (equal to 0.05 in the £) resulting in an increase of this amount (i.e. from £0.20 to £0.25 per £ of capital employed) in the return on capital employed.

Table 7.2 Inter-firm comparison

	Firm A	Firm B
ROCE	39.0%	39.0%
Margin on sales	13.0%	6.5%
Capital turnover	3.0	6.0

Differences in these ratios obtained by different firms can also arise because of the commercial and financial strategies adopted by different firms, as shown in Table 7.2. In the case of Firm A, a higher added value is reflected by a lower turnover of capital compared with Firm B, which adopts a strategy of lower added value (more price competitive) and a higher turnover of capital. Both firms achieve the same rate of return on capital employed.

FINANCIAL STABILITY

In order to prosper, firms need, in addition to earning an adequate rate of return, to maintain a degree of financial stability. Measures of this can be derived from the balance sheet by calculating both the current ratio (sometimes referred to as the 'solvency ratio') and the liquidity ratio (sometimes referred to as the 'acid test ratio'). The current ratio is the division of the current assets by the current liabilities, and is expressed as a whole number. This value should be greater than 1, indicating that the firm has more short-term assets than short-term liabilities. The liquidity ratio is the division of the 'liquid' assets (current assets less stocks, or debtors plus cash) by the current liabilities. Debtors are considered a liquid asset, as they are constantly being settled and being replaced with new debt in the form of current deliveries to customers. This value should also be greater than 1, indicating that the firm is liquid, i.e it can meet all its short-term liabilities as they arise. In practice, firms can operate quite adequately on liquidity ratios marginally less than 1.

Table 7.3 illustrates the accounts and ratios of a firm for three years. The ROCE shows a satisfactory increase over the period; in year 2 this is due solely to the increase in the margin on sales (MOS). However, in year 3 the decline in the capital turnover (CT) has offset the increase in the MOS, and the ROCE, while increasing to 30 per cent, would have been 36 per cent had the CT been maintained at 2. The company remains solvent during the three years, as evidenced by the current ratio, but the policy of increasing the investment in stock (as a proportion of the current assets) has introduced a degree of illiquidity in years 2 and 3. This is not a particular problem as, although the firm has less liquid assets than liabilities, the creditors will not all fall due to be paid at the same time. Thus the firm will be able to operate without any undue cash flow problems at these levels of illiquidity. However, should they fall below 0.7 then cash flow problems would certainly arise.

The return on shareholders' funds increases to 70 per cent due to the increase in the level of gearing, i.e. proportionally more of the total capital is provided by loan capital. The return is enhanced because the return obtained on the loan capital element is greater than its cost, and because this surplus accrues to the equity shareholders, as shown in Table 7.4. Thus

Table 7.3 Three years' accounts and ratios

	£000		
	Year 1	Year 2	Year 3
Fixed assets	800	1300	2400
Current assets:			
Stocks	200	400	800
Debtors	400	400	800
Current liabilities	(400)	(600)	(1000)
Net assets	1,000	1,500	3,000
Loan capital	500	500	2000
Shareholders' funds	500	1,000	1,000
Sales	2,000	3,000	5,000
Profit	200	400	900
Interest	50	50	200
Profit before tax	150	350	700
ROCE	20.0%	26.6%	30.0%
Margin on sales	10.0%	13.3%	18.0%
Capital turnover	2.0	2.0	1.7
Return on shareholders' funds	30.0%	35.0%	70.0%
Gearing	50.0%	33.3%	66.6%
Current ratio	1.5	1.3	1.6
Liquidity ratio	1.0	0.7	0.8

the risk incurred by introducing debt into the capital structure is compensated by the increased return.

As has previously been explained, the rate of profitability does not occur, or change, in a random fashion, but arises due to the interaction of a number of factors, each of which also arises due to the interaction of a number of other factors. Thus the identification of these factors in a particular business enables management to identify, and thus monitor, the causes of changes in the rate of profitability.

In assessing the profitability of a business it is necessary to appreciate that there is a minimum rate of return that must be earned, and which differs from business to business. Although the rate of return can be analysed to show how and why it has occurred at a particular level, the determination as to whether the rate is adequate is not entirely subjective. This has to do with risk, and the risk exposure for businesses is different and individual.

At a simple level, risk is about liquidity and realisability of investments. It follows that a deposit in a savings account is a relatively risk-free

Table 7.4 Effect of gearing on shareholders' returns

	£000		
	Year 1	*Year 2*	*Year 3*
Loan capital	500	500	2,000
Equity capital	500	1,000	1,000
	1,000	1,500	3,000
Profit	200	400	900
earned by:			
loan capital	100	133	600
equity capital	100	267	300
Loan capital:			
cost (interest)	50	50	200
surplus	50	83	400
Equity capital	100	267	300
Total available for equity			
shareholders	150	350	700
Return on equity capital	30.0%	35.0%	70.0%

investment. Although the return (rate of interest) is low, in comparison with other investment opportunities, there is complete flexibility and the investor can alter the nature of the investment as he perceives the nature of the risk changing. At the other end of the scale, investment in business enterprise is probably the least realisable area of investment and it follows that the rate of return must compensate for this increased level of risk. It is also self-evident that some enterprises are inherently more risky than others – manufacturing capital goods compared with manufacturing consumer goods, for example, and therefore their rate of return must compensate for the degree of risk peculiar to that business.

In assessing the rate of return for a particular business it is necessary to construct a risk profile that allows for all the risk present in that particular business, not the least of which will be the risk attaching to the level of inflation that the business is experiencing.

RATIO ANALYSIS

Primary ratios

Prime ratio

The prime ratio is the profitability ratio, which is the profit expressed as a percentage of the capital employed. Care must be exercised when calculating this ratio to ensure that the definitions of profit and capital are consistent, particularly where any form of inter-firm comparison is being made. In this context profit is defined as profit before taxation and interest on loan capital, but excluding overdrafts (operating profit); capital employed is defined as the total of fixed assets and net current assets, which are current assets less current liabilities, including overdrafts.

The rate of return occurs because of the interaction of two other primary ratios: the margin on sales, and the capital turnover ratio.

Margin on sales

This is the average margin achieved on sales in a business after deducting costs. Changes in this ratio are caused by changes in prices, costs, sales mix and, potentially the most important, changes in productivity.

Capital turnover ratio

Possibly the least understood relationship in the assessment of business performance is that between the value of sales and the amount of capital employed. It is not possible, due to the individual characteristics of businesses, to formulate a standard for this relationship but it should be obvious that a restriction exists in terms of the value of sales that can be financed by a given amount of capital. The ratio expresses the value of sales that have been generated from each £1 of capital employed.

Given that each £1 of sales earns a margin on sales, it follows that the level of profitability will be equal to the multiplication of the capital turnover ratio by the ratio for the margin on sales.

The implications for improving profitability are, therefore, to maximise both of the primary ratios – capital turnover and margin on sales.

It is probable that in most businesses it is the former that is capable of the most significant rate of improvement, as the operation of capital, particularly working capital, at optimum levels is a matter of policy. Improvements in the sales margin have to be made in the competitive market arena and often these pressures severely limit the scope for management action. The nature of the business will, to a large extent, dictate the amount of capital investment but there remains considerable scope, within these constraints, for the effective and efficient optimization of capital employment.

The conclusion that some businesses require larger capital bases than others lies in the nature of the particular business. For example, a construction company, or a manufacturer of heavy capital equipment, will require a large investment in fixed assets and their working capital requirements need to be sufficient to cover the long time period required to complete the product. Conversely, a retailing company may be able to operate on a lower investment in fixed assets and with lower working capital requirements than for a manufacturing company. Subject to the individual risk profile, it follows that the margin on sales must be such as to compensate for the differences in capital turnover ratios.

Profitability ratios

Changes that have occurred in the margin on sales will be due to a combination of the following reasons.

Contribution percentage

This represents the gross margin (and is sometimes defined as the gross profit) earned on the sale of all products. Changes in the overall (average) percentage can be due to a number of factors:

1 Increases in variable costs not being passed on to customers will cause a decline in the ratio. A continuation of this trend, without a compensatory increase in sales volume, would result in a lower fund from which fixed costs (overheads) can be funded, with the resultant lowering of the overall margin on sales.
2 Increases in selling prices at a rate higher than increases in variable costs will result in an increased average percentage.

Sales mix

Changes in the contribution percentage can be caused by a change in the mix of products sold. An increase in the share of total sales taken by products with a low contribution margin will result in a fall in the overall percentage. Conversely an increase in the sales of those products with a higher contribution ratio will result in an improvement in the overall ratio. It is important that management are aware of the contributions earned on each of their products, and of their relative proportions of the product mix. Arguably, it is equally important that they are aware of any changes that are taking place.

Fixed costs

It follows that if costs are fixed (in relation to sales), then as a percentage of sales, from one period to another, this ratio should fall if sales increase. If this ratio reveals a tendency to rise then this can be considered an early warning sign of impending bankruptcy, as inevitably if the trend continues then profit margins will be eroded.

In most firms the largest fixed cost element is salaries and wages, and analysis usually reveals wage increases to be the prime cause of a declining trend. Diagnosis often provides its own prescription!

Productivity ratios

To understand the measures of productivity it is necessary to understand the purpose of employment: to use the collective skills and energies of the work-force to earn profits. The profits are earned from output (sales), and the measures of productivity are, therefore, measures of the relationship between inputs (numbers of employees) and the output of the organisation (sales). In this context it is important to appreciate that the expression work-force includes all employees, from the chairman to the junior office boy. One of the commonest misconceptions of productivity is that it relates only to manual workers. Not only is this not so, but productivity is a very effective means of measuring the effectiveness of the administrative functions.

The number of productivity ratios that can be calculated is limited only by the analyst's imagination, and the usefulness of the ratio provided. The following are indicative of the type of ratio that can be calculated.

Sales per employee

This measures the value of sales generated by each employee in the period under review. Increases reflect either the increased productivity of each and every employee (bearing in mind that there will be different numbers of employees employed in each period), or the effects of increases in selling prices. In order to assess productivity more accurately, it may be advisable to produce a non-financial measure based on a physical measurement of output, or to produce a ratio such as the following one.

Sales per £ remuneration

Given that both sales prices and rates of remuneration are subject to price change, this ratio examines the relative value of any productivity changes resulting from changes in the values of the input and output factors. Increases in the ratio are indications of improving productivity, whereas a decline indicates either that too many people are employed, or that they are being paid too much. Once again, a diagnosis that provides its own prescription!

Profit per employee

If the measure of productivity is the use of employment to earn profits, then the ultimate arbiter must be the profit earned by each employee. Should this ratio be increasing, despite declines in other productivity ratios, this can be explained by the containment of non-employment costs. Improvements in the other productivity ratios would then produce further improvements in this ratio. It cannot be emphasised too strongly that this ratio must, at the very least, be a static one; a declining trend would bode ill for the future of the firm.

Performance ratios

Performance ratios indicate the productivity (in financial terms) of the assets of the business in terms of generating sales – which is, to state the obvious, the purpose of making the investment. Investment that does not produce revenue cannot produce profit and is, therefore, an investment that should not have been made. The use of these ratios will indicate those areas of investment where liquidation and reinvestment will improve overall profitability.

Measurement of the sales/total assets (capital turnover) ratio reveals only the average performance, and in order to identify areas requiring attention, an analysis is required. The first step is to analyse the total investment into its two main areas:

- long-term (fixed assets);
- short-term (working capital or net current assets).

Sales/fixed assets

The fixed asset turnover can be calculated in total and for each asset category. Indeed it can be calculated for groups of assets and for individual assets within categories. Obviously the nature of the business will dictate the extent to which this analysis is appropriate or necessary. What the ratio indicates is the extent to which productivity (in terms of sales generated) is increasing or decreasing.

Care needs to be exercised in interpreting this ratio, as two factors tend towards an increasing ratio:

1 **Depreciation** The writing down of an asset naturally gives rise to a tendency to an increasing ratio, and a check should be made that additions to fixed assets are at least equal to the depreciation write-off.
2 **Changing prices** Increases in selling prices will give an indication of an increasing ratio, compared with the historical written-down value of the assets. Care must be taken to adjust for any increases in selling prices, possibly by indexing the book value of assets by the same factor. Where it is possible, it may be preferable to use an output measure that has a physical characteristic.

Sales/working capital (net current assets)

This gives an overall assessment of the performance of the working capital investment, but more significant management control can be exercised through the calculation of the ratios for the main constituents of working capital – stocks and debtors.

1 **Sales/stocks**   Arguably the most important management ratio, this indicates the level of investment in stocks relative to sales. A decreasing ratio is indicative of over-investment in these areas. It is probably true to state that no other area offers such scope for improvement. To be fully effective, ratios should be calculated for each category of investment, e.g. raw materials, work-in-progress and finished goods. In order to assess the effectiveness of the ratio the optimum stock-holding relative to the particular business should be calculated and compared with the ratio which reveals the *actual* level of stockholding.
2 **Sales/debtors**   This ratio reveals the actual level of credit being extended to customers, and can be compared with the terms of trade. An increasing ratio indicates a lack of credit control and the diversion of investment from more productive areas.

   The control of the total investment in working capital is of paramount importance, because over-investment in this area deprives other, more important areas, of necessary funds. This is of particular importance to manufacturing concerns where the need for funds for investment in fixed assets (which produce the products on which profit is earned) is often desperate.
3 **Sales/creditors**   This ratio reveals the extent to which creditors (current liabilities) are being used to fund the investment in stocks and debtors. Inefficient investment in these areas can be 'masked' by an extension of suppliers' credit, and it is important that this ratio also shows a stable trend. If it increases, that is an indication of a further extension of credit, which bodes ill for the future financial stability of the firm.

Stability ratios

The effect of pursuing a policy of maximisation of the profitability, productivity and performance ratios could be the introduction of an element of instability into the financial structure of the concern. Calculation of the stability ratios (current and liquidity) will monitor the situation, but where a firm is solvent – i.e., it has a solvency ratio greater than 1, but is illiquid – i.e., it has a liquidity ratio of less than 1, this will be due to excessive investment in stocks. This can be measured by calculating the following ratio.

Stock/net current assets

Should a concern be solvent but have a liquidity ratio of less than 1, then the cause lies in the extent of the investment in stocks. By calculating the percentage of stock to working capital (net current assets), the cause of the illiquidity can be appreciated. Where the percentage exceeds 100, then the company is utilising short-term borrowings (trade creditors) to finance stock investment. Whereas this is an admirable policy from the point of view of improving the performance ratios, it is an obvious cause of financial instability and if pursued indiscriminately could lead to the financial collapse of the firm.

ILLUSTRATION

The reports shown in Table 7.5 are used to illustrate the calculation and interpretation of ratios in order to form an opinion of the performance of a firm over the period. The process of analysis can begin with an assessment of the growth over the four years. this can be done by using year 1 as a base of 100 and expressing the following years as a percentage of that base, for each of the main elements, as shown in Table 7.6. It can be observed that capital employed has grown by some 52.0 per cent, compared with a growth of some 41.5 per cent in sales, indicating a fall in the efficiency of the utilisation of capital during the period. On the other hand, operating profit has increased by some 70.2 per cent, indicating an improvement in both the return on capital employed and the profit margin to sales over the period. As the profit before taxation has increased by 53.5 per cent compared with the growth in shareholders' funds of 29.4 per cent, the return on shareholders' funds has also increased. This is partly due to the improvement in the return on capital employed, and this improvement has been enhanced by the introduction of loan capital (debt) into the capital structure. The degree of gearing is quite modest:

	19X1	19X2	19X3	19X4
Gearing (debt as a percentage of capital employed)	0.0	5.5	11.5	14.9

Nonetheless, this modest use of debt capital has enhanced the shareholders' earnings.

An examination of the cash flow reports reveals that the cash position has deteriorated by some £193,000, despite cash flows generated from trading of £1,720,000. This is reduced to £1,086,000 when the additional investment in working capital has been deducted. Payments of interest, dividends and taxation further reduce the figure to £200,000. This is the amount of cash generated by trading operations during the four years. It compares with reported operating profits of £1,373,000. It is from this

Table 7.5 Five years' financial reports

Balance sheet as at 31 March	£000			
	19X1	*19X2*	*19X3*	*19X4*
Fixed assets	1,417	1,615	1,723	1,946
Current assets				
Stocks	739	859	987	1,123
Debtors	647	636	782	879
	1,386	1,495	1,769	2,002
Less current liabilities				
Creditors	735	698	582	749
Overdraft	277	342	456	512
Taxation	111	128	165	140
Dividends	47	54	62	65
	1,170	1,222	1,265	1,466
Net current assets	216	273	504	536
Total assets less current liabilities	1,633	1,888	2,227	2,482
Less loans		103	257	369
Total net assets	1,633	1,785	1,970	2,113
Financed by:				
Issued ordinary shares	536	558	608	608
Reserves	1,090	1,183	1,308	1,451
Revaluation reserve	7	34	34	34
Share premium		10	20	20
Shareholders' funds	1,633	1,785	1,970	2,113

Table 7.5 continued

Profit and loss account for the year ended 31 March	£000			
	19X1	*19X2*	*19X3*	*19X4*
Sales	3,070	3,555	3,987	4,345
Operating profit[a]	258	299	379	437
Less loan interest		12	27	41
Profit before taxation	258	287	352	396
Taxation	99	115	142	163
Profit after taxation	159	172	210	233
Dividends	71	79	85	90
Retained profit	88	93	125	143
[a]After charging:				
Depreciation	47	82	103	115
Employees	526	556	589	623
Remuneration (£000)	863	949	1,053	1,182

Cash flow report year ended 31 March	£000			
	19X1	*19X2*	*19X3*	*19X4*
Operating profit	258	299	379	437
Add depreciation	47	82	103	115
Less increase (decrease in working capital	32	146	390	66
Net cash flow from operating activities	273	235	92	486
Servicing of finance				
Interest paid		12	27	41
Dividends paid	71	72	77	87
	202	151	(12)	358
Taxation paid	108	98	105	188
	94	53	(117)	170
Investing activities				
Purchase of fixed assets	52	253	211	338
Net cash inflow (outflow) before financing	42	(200)	(328)	(168)
Financing				
Loan capital		103	154	112
Share capital		32	60	
Increase (decrease) in cash	42	(65)	(114)	(56)

Table 7.6 Growth analysis

	19X1	19X2	19X3	19X4
Capital employed	100.0	115.6	136.4	152.0
Sales	100.0	115.8	129.9	141.5
Operating profit	100.0	104.2	146.9	170.2
Shareholders' funds	100.0	109.3	120.6	129.4
Profit before taxation	100.0	111.2	136.4	153.5

amount, plus any additional loan and share capital, that the long-term investment in fixed assets is to be funded. The additional share capital of £92,000 and loan capital of £369,000 is clearly inadequate, and the shortfall in the current cash resource (overdraft) becomes a matter of concern. Additional fixed asset investment amounted to £854,000, of which £193,000 was provided from overdraft facilities.

The gross investment was in increased working capital of £823,000, of which £189,000 was financed by trade creditors. This is also a contributory factor in the decrease in cash resources.

Table 7.7 Stability ratios

	19X1	19X2	19X3	19X4
Current ratio	1.2	1.2	1.4	1.4
Liquidity ratio	0.6	0.5	0.6	0.6
Acid test ratio (1)	0.9	0.9	1.3	1.2
Acid test ratio (2)	0.7	0.7	1.0	0.9
Stock/net current assets %	150.0	140.0	103.0	107.0

The quality of these financial policies can be assessed by calculating the appropriate ratios, the first of which might be the stability ratios as shown in Table 7.7. The firm is clearly solvent, as in each year current assets exceed current liabilities. However, the liquidity (acid test) ratio will examine its ability to pay (as opposed to settle) its short-term liabilities. The ratio indicates an uncomfortable degree of illiquidity, but a stricter assessment can be made by excluding both taxation and dividend creditors (which are only paid once or twice a year) and also by excluding the overdraft (acid test ratio (1)), which while technically a current liability, because it is repayable on demand, does not, in the normal course of events, require repayment from current assets. In the latter two years the firm is liquid and during the earlier period the degree of illiquidity was only marginal. The position is still satisfactory if both dividend and taxation creditors are included in the calculation (acid test ratio (2)).

The reason for the difference between the current ratio and the liquidity ratio is explained by the ratio of stocks to working capital (net current assets). It is important to understand that this latter figure is provided by the firm from its capital employed and is then supplemented by short-term finance, i.e. creditors, to provide the investment fund for debtors and stocks. It should be self-evident that where the investment in stocks exceeds the value of working capital, then there will be a level of illiquidity.

It should be appreciated that overdrafts are included in current liabilities because they are technically repayable on demand. In fact many firms use overdraft facilities as part of their everyday capital, and ratio calculations have more credibility if the overdraft is treated in this way and added to capital employed. Note that if this method is used then the interest on overdrafts should be added back to operating profit in order to obtain an accurate calculation of the return on capital employed. In this illustration, no adjustment has been made for the overdraft.

Table 7.8 Primary ratios

	19X1	19X2	19X3	19X4
Return on capital employed %	15.8	15.8	17.0	17.6
Profit margins %	8.4	8.4	9.5	10.1
Capital turnover	1.9	1.9	1.8	1.7

The primary ratios are set out in Table 7.8. Earlier observations are confirmed, in that the ROCE and profit margins have improved while there has been a deterioration in the rate of capital turnover, which is in the order of 10 per cent over the period. As has previously been stressed, it is not the absolute value of the ratio that is important but the rate of change that occurs. In this latter case a fall of 0.2 per cent from 1.9 per cent is a fall of 10 per cent! The reasons for this will be determined by calculating a series of performance ratios from the balance sheet values.

Table 7.9 Productivity ratios

	19X1	19X2	19X3	19X4
Sales per employee (£000)	5.8	6.4	6.8	7.0
Sales per £ remuneration	3.6	3.8	3.8	3.7
Profit per employee (£000)	0.5	0.5	0.6	0.7

Because published financial reports do not include details of costs, but only report sales and operating profits, the reasons for the change in the profit margin ratio cannot be determined. However, the reports do include details of employees and their remuneration, and these can be used to calculate a number of productivity ratios (Table 7.9). While apparently improving satisfactorily, it should be remembered that sales have the benefits of price inflation, while numbers of employees do not. The improvement could be overstated if the degree of price inflation is significant – when has this not been so in the United Kingdom in recent memory? The calculation of the sales per £ of remuneration will, to a very large extent, remove this distortion. A very different picture is revealed, in that productivity has been maintained during the period but has not improved significantly. The calculation of the profit per employee reveals a dramatic improvement which suggests that the improvement in profit margins has arisen due to the containment of non-employee-related costs.

Table 7.10 Performance ratios

	19X1	19X2	19X3	19X4
Sales/fixed assets	2.2	2.2	2.3	2.2
Sales/stocks	4.2	4.1	4.0	3.9
Sales/debtors	4.7	5.6	5.1	4.9
Sales/trade creditors	4.2	5.1	6.9	5.8

The calculation of the performance ratios will indicate the causes of the decline in the utilisation of capital employed. This indicates that the productivity of fixed assets (both old and new investments) has been maintained, and it is evident from the financial reports that the amount of investment has exceeded depreciation provisions. It can be concluded with confidence that this maintenance of productivity (in terms of generating sales) has been made in real terms, i.e. without the influence of inflation.

Table 7.11 Working capital ratios in months

	19X1	19X2	19X3	19X4
Sales/stocks	2.9	2.9	3.0	3.1
Sales/debtors	2.6	2.1	2.4	2.4
Sales/trade creditors	2.9	2.4	1.7	2.1

The other performance ratios relate to working capital. The ratios can also be expressed in terms of time, which helps to make their interpretation easier. Expressed as months (by dividing the ratios into twelve), they are as shown in Table 7.11. The analysis shows that stockholding has increased but that credit control has improved, and that less dependence is being placed on trade credit as a source of short-term finance. The increase in stocks is clearly the primary reason for the increase in overdrafts noted from the review of the cash flow reports, and while credit control has been tightened, the reduction in the use of trade credit may well have been at the instigation of the creditors themselves.

It is worth noting that the increase in stocks of 0.2 represents some £87,000 and that this amount has been funded from the overdraft. More importantly, it is the primary cause of the decline in the efficient utilisation of capital employed.

CONCLUSION

The use of ratios as a management tool is extremely important and it enables quite subtle changes in the financial structure and performance of a business to be detected at an early stage and to be either encouraged or corrected. It must be emphasised that the technique is one of trend analysis, and that a single series of ratios at a given date is of only limited value. In order to make correct interpretations a trend must be established and constantly updated.

Only a limited number of ratios have been mentioned and each concern can, and should, establish its own profile of meaningful ratios. The general rule is that if a relationship can be established between two variables, and control exercised, then that is a useful ratio.

Lord Weinstock, chairman of GEC, is thought to be an advocate of ratio analysis and it is believed that the performance of the many subsidiaries of his highly successful company are monitored and controlled by the use of the following seven key ratios:

1 return on capital employed;
2 profit margin to sales;
3 capital turnover;
4 sales/stocks;
5 sales/fixed assets;
6 sales per £ of remuneration;
7 profit per employee.

The first three comprise the prime and primary ratios and not only measure the progress of the ROCE, but identify the causes of any change. The fourth reports on an area where it is all too easy to make unnecessary investment in the pursuit of profit. The fifth is of particular importance to manufacturing concerns, because it is the area of investment from which sales are derived via the manufacture of products. The last two measure the productivity and profitability of the crucial area of employment. It is not difficult to imagine that in the event of an untoward trend developing in any of these areas, then further analysis of the appropriate subsidiary ratios will enable a diagnosis of the particular problems to be made and the appropriate strategies devised for their correction.

Each firm will need to devise its own profile of ratios and decide the frequency with which they should be monitored. The consequence of such an approach is that attention is directed not towards absolute values but towards relationships, and more particularly, towards the changes that are occurring in those relationships.

KEY LEARNING POINTS

- **This chapter has considered the identification of the prime ratio of business performance and of its constituents, as well as their relationship and their calculation and the reasons for changes arising in them.**
- **An explanation has been provided of the effect of gearing, introducing loan capital into the firm's financial structure, and the benefits that accrue to the owners of the business, the ordinary shareholders, from such arrangements.**
- **Measures of financial stability have been examined, together with an explanation of the causes of financial instability.**
- **Those ratios necessary for the further analysis and explanation of changes arising in the primary ratios have been identified.**

CASE STUDY

Analysis of accounts

Prepare a detailed analysis of the accounts for the three years to 31 December 19X2 utilising as many of the ratios illustrated in this chapter as possible, and, after giving due consideration to the detail available in these accounts, any other ratios that you feel would be useful.

Interpretation of accounts

Prepare a report for Peter French based on your analysis, identifying the strengths and weaknesses of his business and suggesting any steps that your analysis indicates are necessary for its future success.

Part II

Management accounting

Chapter 8

Product costs

INTRODUCTION

Determination of product costs is important for the purposes of management control and has implications for a number of crucial decisions: setting selling prices, deciding whether to accept or reject orders, monitoring productivity, changing production methods and continuing (or discontinuing) the manufacture of products.

However, the determination of these costs is only one element in such decisions, and a number of other factors will also need to be considered, such as the nature of the costs, whether or not they are variable or fixed, and whether or not they are future costs or sunk costs.

A matter of prime importance is the control of the total costs of an organisation, and consideration of the process of obtaining and controlling individual product costs should not detract from this primary responsibility.

COSTING

As a first stage it is necessary to consider the process involved in determining product costs. This is the accounting process that allocates and apportions all of the total costs within the organisation to individual products or services, in order to ascertain the cost of the provision of those products or services.

There are two broad approaches to costing: first, where the costs are 'added' at each stage of the production process (known as job costing), and second, where the cost of producing a quantity of the same product is ascertained and then divided by the quantity produced (process costing). All costing systems will fall into one or the other of these mechanisms, although some, more complex, operations will utilise both approaches. For instance, a road transport operation carrying freight will determine its costs per tonne mile, that is the cost of transporting one tonne of a customer's goods for one mile. This is an example of the process approach. It is not the cost of travelling one mile, but the cost of carrying a customer's goods for one mile – a subtle but important difference. A firm of solicitors or professional accountants would adopt the job approach by determining the cost of the provision of a service to a particular client, the services offered being similar but different for each individual client.

ELEMENTS OF COST

In order to calculate individual product costs, a number of steps are required. The approach is universal, but such is the individuality of firms that the approach will differ in detail from one firm to another. However, it is most important to understand that this process cannot be abridged; attempts to 'short-cut' the process will result in an inaccurate picture of product costs.

First, costs are categorised as to their function into direct costs and indirect costs as depicted in Figure 8.1.

Direct costs

These comprise any cost that is incurred in respect of a particular product or service. If that product is not produced or the service is not provided, then the cost will not be incurred. They will usually comprise:

- direct materials;
- direct wages;
- direct expenses.

The total of the direct costs is defined as the 'prime cost' of a product or service. An example of indirect expenses could be the charges incurred by a firm of solicitors transacting a property conveyance for a client.

It should be appreciated that both materials and wages will be provided generally by the firm and utilised over a range of products. However, if a product is not produced, then that material or those wages will be utilised in respect of a different product.

Indirect costs

These are any costs that are not direct costs and which arise as a result of the existence of the firm and its function in producing products or providing services. Examples are rent and rates of premises, administrative salaries, heating and lighting costs, etc.

The indirect costs will first be categorised into their respective functions:

- works or factory indirect costs;
- administration indirect costs;
- selling and distribution indirect costs.

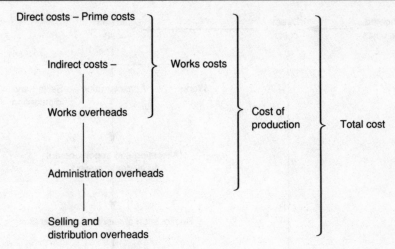

Figure 8.1 Functions of cost

Each of these functions will have similar categories of costs, e.g. indirect wages and salaries, rent and rates, insurances etc.

ALLOCATION AND APPORTIONMENT

In order to attribute costs to individual products or services, it is necessary to allocate and apportion them within the departmental structure of a firm. It is at this stage that the individuality of the organisation is reflected in its cost structure, and no matter how similar the products produced by different firms, the organisational structure is likely to be different. It is this that can cause differences to arise in the cost of the provision of a product or service.

It must be appreciated that the total of the individual costs of the output of a firm cannot be different from the total costs of that firm. The costing process is one of allocating the *total* costs (both direct and indirect) to the individual products or services. The firm must determine its organisational structure and identify all of its cost centres and departments, both productive and non-productive. This process must be carried out in considerable detail (Figure 8.2). Once it has been completed then the process of allocation and apportionment can be undertaken. This is achieved by means of an overhead allocation sheet of the type shown in Table 8.1. Each category of indirect overhead (expense) is then allocated or apportioned (i.e. shared out) between the various departments on an equitable basis that will reflect the incurring of that expense by each of the departments.

The difference between allocation and apportionment is somewhat indistinct. Allocation can be assumed to be the division of an expense between two or more cost centres on the basis of the estimated relative usage by

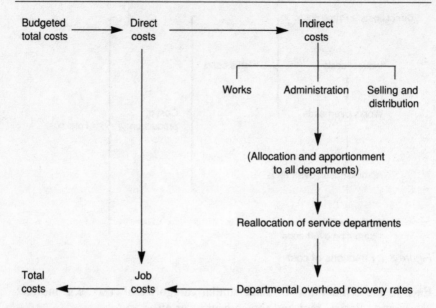

Figure 8.2 Cost recovery process

Table 8.1 Overhead allocation sheet

		Department					
Overheads £000	Total	P_1	P_2	P_3	S_1	S_2	S_3
Wages	120	40	20	10	20	15	15
Salaries	60	10		5	15	15	15
Rent and rates	40	14	8	12	3	2	1
Insurances	20	5	4	2	2	4	3
Depreciation	60	25	15	15			5
Power	30	10	12	8			
Maintenance – buildings	10	3	2	2	2	1	0
Maintenance – plant	15	3	4	5	2		1
Welfare expenses	30	5	7	4	6	3	5
Totals	385	115	72	63	50	40	45

those departments, or where an indirect expense is incurred by only one department. Apportionment is the distribution of an indirect expense, incurred generally by the firm as a whole, by means of a predetermined formula. The choice of that formula is subjective, and this is another aspect that can make the determination of product costs different between similar firms producing similar products.

Examples of bases of allocation and apportionment are:

- space-related, e.g. used for rent and rates;
- employee-related, used for personnel costs;
- activity-related, used for power etc.;
- cost-related, used for depreciation.

In the previous illustration, the bases used could have been:

- Wages and salaries – allocated directly.
- Rent and rates and maintenance of buildings – apportioned on the basis of area.
- Insurances and depreciation – apportioned on the basis of cost of plant in each department.
- Power – apportioned on the basis of the output of each department.
- Welfare expenses – apportioned on the numbers of employees in each department.
- Maintenance of plant – this might have been allocated or apportioned on the basis of the cost of the plant in each department, or might have used a combination of both methods.

Once all the indirect expenses of the firm have been allocated and apportioned to the cost centres, consideration can be given to 'recovering' those indirect expenses (overheads) to the products and services produced by the cost centres. This is the essential step which 'shares out' the indirect expenses of each department to all of the products produced by that department in the most equitable manner, giving due regard to the different use that each product will make of the resources of the department as represented by the indirect costs. An example of this can be seen from consideration of work done for different clients in a solicitors' office. The more work done for one client, as opposed to another, the greater will be the charge for overheads to that client, reflecting the greater use of the resources purchased by the overheads.

REALLOCATION OF SERVICE DEPARTMENTS' INDIRECT OVERHEADS

A cursory consideration given to almost any firm will reveal that some of its departments are 'service' departments, whose resources individual products and services do not utilise and which exist to provide a support function to the producing departments and cost centres. Indeed, some of the service departments will exist to provide support services to other service departments. Before the process of overhead recovery can be addressed, the costs of the service departments must be reallocated or reapportioned to the production departments. This is essentially the same process that was undertaken with the allocation and apportionment.

Even in the smallest of firms, the reallocation of service departments can be a complex proposition, particularly where some service departments provide services to one another. In these cases the reallocation process is made by means of mathematical formulae, but the end result is the same, in that the costs allocated and apportioned to these departments are reallocated to the production departments, and the end result is that all of the indirect overhead costs of the firm are allocated to the production departments.

An illustration of the reallocation of service department costs from the previous example could be:

- Service department S_1 provides services equally to all other departments, including the other service departments.
- Service department S_2 provides 10 per cent of its output to S_3 and the remainder equally to the production departments.
- Service department S_3 provides equally to the three production departments.

The process of reallocation will commence with S_1 which services all departments, followed by S_2 which services S_3, and finally with S_3 which only services the production departments as shown in Table 8.2.

Table 8.2 Reallocation of service department indirect costs

		Department					
	Total	P_1	P_2	P_3	S_1	S_2	S_3
Totals allocated £000	385	115	72	63	50	40	45
Dept. S_1		10	10	10	(50)	10	10
Dept. S_2		15	15	15		(50)	5
Dept. S_3		20	20	20			(60)
Totals	385	160	117	108			

OVERHEAD RECOVERY

The next stage in the process of determining product total costs is to 'recover' the departmental indirect costs to the individual products or services.

The selection of the recovery mechanism is the most important element in the costing process. The choice of an inappropriate recovery mechanism will result in the attribution of a department's indirect costs to products being distorted. Any attempt to short circuit this process, by 'banding' departments together, will also lead to distortion of the product costs. In either case, the total indirect overheads of the firm will be attributed to the output, but different results will be obtained by differing methods. The process is necessarily complex, and considerable attention must be paid both to the detail of the organisation and to the nature of the operations in the cost centre.

The recovery mechanism should be the one that effects the most equitable distribution of the overheads to the products or services representing the output of the department, and it will essentially reflect the manufacturing or operational process within the department that materially alters the product or service from its previous state.

The common methods of overhead recovery are:

- as a percentage of the direct material cost of the product;
- as a percentage of the direct departmental labour cost of the product;
- as a rate per direct departmental labour hour;
- as a rate per direct departmental machine hour.

The choice of one of the above will be influenced solely by the nature of the productive process within the department. If the essential difference between products is the time that is spent on the product, e.g. repairing a motor car, then a labour hour rate would be the most appropriate. If, however, there were differences in the rates paid to the direct labour within the department, then this might be inappropriate and a plusage to the labour cost might be more equitable, e.g. in a car repair shop where there were a number of different types of skilled and semi-skilled employees, paid at different rates. To attribute overheads on the basis of hours might produce an inequitable distribution of overheads to those jobs that utilised the lower rate of skills. If the process within the department were essentially a mechanical one, then the use of a machine hour rate would be chosen.

Of course, there are situations in which neither machine hour, labour hour nor labour costs are appropriate, e.g. a car bodywork paint-spray shop, and in this case the use of direct material cost as a basis for recovering overheads could be selected; even though this might not be the 'best' method, it could be the one that will produce the next-best result.

For example, assume that the following data relate to the previous example of overhead allocation. Department P_1 is labour-intensive, and overheads are to be recovered on the basis of labour hours, department P_2 is automated, and overhead recovery is on the basis of machine hours, and the overheads of department P_3 are to be recovered by utilising a rate per labour hour.

Budgeted hours and costs are:

- Department P_1: 40,000 direct labour hours.
- Department P_2: 10,000 machine hours.
- Department P_3: £30,000 direct labour cost.

- **Department P_1** Overheads/labour hours = £160,000/40,000 = £4.00 per direct labour hour.
- **Department P_2** Overheads/machine hours = £117,000/10,000 = £11.70 per machine hour.
- **Department P_3** Overheads/labour cost × 100 = £108,000/£30,000 × 100 = 360 per cent.

Thus the overhead recovery rates are:

- Department P_1:   £4.00 per direct labour hour.
- Department P_2:   £11.70 per machine hour.
- Department P_3:   360 per cent of direct labour cost.

Some authorities recommend that a further method is that of an addition to prime (direct) cost, i.e. the total of direct materials and direct labour cost, but it is difficult to envisage any circumstances in practice that would benefit from the adoption of this technique. Almost all circumstances that can be envisaged would benefit from the adoption of a recovery mechanism, of one or other of the constituents of prime cost, rather than the plurality of the two.

Underpinning any system of costing there must be a detailed accounting recording system covering the receipt and issue of stores (materials) and the recording of time spent on jobs. It is essential that these are operated at optimum levels of efficiency if the resulting cost information is to have an acceptable degree of utility.

COMPILING PRODUCT COSTS

Once the election as to the mechanisms of overhead recovery has been made, then the process of job cost compilation can be undertaken. This process adds the costs at each stage of production to the previous totals, commencing with the prime (direct) costs. The number of additions that are made to the prime cost in the cost compilation process will depend on the number of 'functions' that the firm is organised into, e.g. works, administration, selling and distribution, etc. It may be that the works is organised into a number of departments and that products go through one or more of these, in which case once the productive process has been completed, the 'works' cost of the product will have been compiled. Further additions will then need to be made to this value in respect of the product's appropriate share of the other categories of indirect overheads, administration, etc.

Administration overhead is usually recovered as a percentage of the works cost of the product or, preferably, as a percentage of the works overhead of the product, to arrive at the total cost of production for the product. A further addition is then made to this in respect of selling and distribution cost. Where this is made as an addition to the cost of production, there is an assumption of homogeneity of selling and delivery of products that is dependent on the relative production costs of products. A moment's reflection will lead to the conclusion that such a situation is the exception rather than the rule and, therefore, that careful consideration needs to be given to the question of the recovery of selling and distribution overheads that will reflect the intrinsic nature of each individual order. It is, generally speaking, as cost effective to obtain an order for a thousand products as it is for one, and, the cost of delivery of a small quantity of product to a distant customer can exceed that for delivery of a large quantity of product to a geographically closer customer. As with all mechanisms of cost recovery, considerable care must be taken to ensure that the outcome reflects the reality of the situation.

Table 8.3 Calculation of works costs

Job no.	FA 342	FA 473	FA 682
Direct materials	£75.00	£68.50	£115.70
Direct labour (£3.00 per hour)	£30.00	£15.00	£51.00
Direct expenses		42.00	
Total direct costs	£105.00	£125.50	£166.70
Machine hours	10	5	7.5
Detailed job costs are:			
Total direct costs	£105.00	£125.50	£166.70
Overheads P_1	£40.00	£20.00	£68.00
Overheads P_2	£117.00	£58.50	£87.75
Overheads P_3	£108.00	£54.00	£183.60
Works costs	£370.00	£258.00	£506.05

Consider three jobs that have been undertaken by the firm which will use the recovery rates previously calculated. Details are shown in Table 8.3. The next stage in the compilation process is to make further additions in respect of administration and selling and distribution overheads. The following details are relative to the previous illustration.

- Total works indirect overheads: £385,000.
- Administration overheads: £135,000.
- Selling and distribution overheads: £85,000.

- Administration overheads are to be recovered as a plusage to works overheads of 35 per cent, and selling and distribution overheads are to be recovered as a plusage of 5 per cent to total production cost.

The product job costs are now as shown in Table 8.4. Thus the process of compilation is completed and the cost of producing these three orders is known.

Two points are worthy of mention. First, for the purpose of valuation for the firm's annual (or periodic) accounts, only the cost of production would be used, according to SSAP 12. In the event that all, or any, of the above jobs were not completed or were not delivered at the valuation date, then all direct costs, together with any works or administration oncost, would be included in the valuation. A second, and much more important, point is that of the total cost calculated for each job, only the direct costs are relevant and all other additions are costs that have been 'attributed' to the jobs. In other words, the process of allocation and apportionment, in each of the cases illustrated, has accounted for the substantial part of the total cost. The process described and illustrated is generically known as 'absorption costing' and it represents the attempt to distribute *all* the costs of the organisation to each unit of output. There is a school of thought that maintains that this process is flawed, and that any attempt to achieve this aim is doomed to failure due to the inherently subjective processes of allocation, apportionment and recovery, all of which, if adopted, might result in differing assessments of product costs. According to this view, the only objective method of determining product costs is to restrict the compilation process to the direct (marginal or variable) costs.

PROCESS COSTING

This approach follows the same procedure as the job cost approach, except that because of the homogeneity of the product all costs, including direct costs, are allocated and apportioned to departments or cost centres, on similar bases to those illustrated, and the process of reallocation of service departments follows the same pattern. However, at this point the process of determining product costs is made by dividing the departmental totals by the output from each of the departments.

Assume that the departmental totals for indirect overheads are the same as in the previous illustration. An example of the process approach is shown in Table 8.5. For cost control purposes the unit costs will be analysed into the constituent elements, i.e. direct materials, wages and overheads. But the approach illustrated is essentially a deductive one, as opposed to the 'additive' approach for job costs.

Table 8.4 Compilation of product costs

Job no.	FA 342	FA 473	FA 682
Works cost	£370.00	£258.00	£586.05
Administration oncost	96.75	46.38	118.77
Cost of production	£462.75	£304.38	£704.82
Selling and distribution oncost	23.14	15.22	35.24
Total cost	£485.89	£319.60	£740.06

Table 8.5 Process costs

£000	Total	P_1	P_2	P_3	S_1	S_2	S_3
Direct materials	1,460	500	350	610			
Direct wages	1,440	450	670	320			
Overheads	385	115	72	63	50	40	45
Service depts.		45	45	45	(50)	(40)	(45)
Totals	3,285	1,110	1,137	1,038			
Output (units)		300	250	590			
Cost per unit		£3.70	£4.15	£1.76			

MANAGEMENT CONTROL OF COSTS

The use of unit cost information by management for control purposes has two purposes: first, to use the data to assess the profitability of the output of the firm, and second, to control the overhead costs of the firm as a whole. In order to do this the actual costs incurred need to be compared, on at least a monthly basis, with the overheads that have been recovered from actual levels of output. These are the totals of the overheads that have been charged to the individual jobs during the period. These will always be different (but only to a small degree) from the actual overheads incurred by the firm, and a major aspect of the cost accountant's function is to continually monitor both the level of overheads incurred against the budgets for those overheads, and to monitor the over- or under-recovery of those overheads from levels of output. It is this latter aspect that indicates the levels of efficiency and productivity within the production functions of the firm.

Figure 8.3 depicts the process graphically. If actual levels of output are above budgeted levels and actual overheads are below budgeted overheads, then there will be an over-recovery of overheads. In other words,

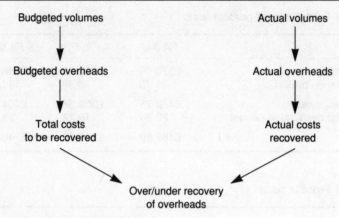

Figure 8.3 Control of overhead costs

the firm will have made more profit than budgeted due to both productive efficiencies and efficient cost control. If, however, actual levels of output are below budgeted levels and actual overheads are above budgeted overheads, then profits will be lower than budget due to the converse reasons of productive inefficiencies and poor cost control.

ILLUSTRATION

Smith Engineering Ltd is a small company that has three production departments A, B and C, and three service departments, X, Y and Z, in addition to administrative and selling and distribution functions.

Service department X's services are exclusive to production department A, Y services all departments, including the other two service departments in equal proportions, and service department Z services the three production departments in the proportions A 25 per cent, B 25 per cent and C 50 per cent.

The budgeted indirect overheads for next year are as follows:

	£000
Works:	
Salaries	60
Power	60
Depreciation: plant	10
Canteen expenses	14
Maintenance: buildings	30
Rent and rates	20
Administration	70
Selling and distribution	45

The following information is in respect of the six departments:

	A	B	C	X	Y	Z
Area (square feet)	1,500	1,500	1,000	500	250	250
Number of employees	20	15	10	15	5	5
Value of buildings (£000)	40	6	80	10	4	10
Value of plant (£000)	20	20	36	4	10	10
Output (000 units)	3	3	2			

There are four supervisors, each paid the same salary. One is in charge of departments A and B, spending 60 per cent of his time in department A; Department X does not have a supervisor, and the others supervise a department each. Departments Y and Z do not use power and department X uses the same amount of power as department C.

Overhead recovery is made on the following bases:

- Department A: material cost %.
- Department B: labour cost %.
- Department C: machine hour rate.
- Administration overheads as a percentage of works cost.
- Selling and distribution overheads as a percentage of the cost of production.

Other relevant details are:

- Budgeted sales: £925,000.
- Budgeted materials: £400,000.
- Budgeted labour cost (Dept. B): £50,000.
- Budgeted machine hours (Dept. C): £10,000.

In order to calculate the selling price for the following enquiry it will be necessary to prepare an overhead allocation sheet to apportion all the works' indirect overheads to the six departments, and to then reapportion the overheads of the service departments to the production departments in accordance with the usage of their services. The bases for the apportionment are subjective and will utilise the information given about the respective departments.

At this stage, the overhead recovery rates for each of the departments can be calculated in accordance with the predetermined bases.

The calculation of the plusage to works cost for the recovery of administration overheads can then be made, followed by the calculation of the plusage to the cost of production in respect of selling and distribution overheads.

Finally, these can be applied to the following data in order to produce an estimate for the enquiry. In practice, if the estimate was accepted by the customer and the order placed, then the estimate would become the standard against which the actual hours and costs incurred on the job would be measured.

- Material required: 10 tonnes at £100.00 per tonne.
- Labour dept. B: 30 hours at £5.00 per hour.
- Machine hours dept. C: 10.
- A profit margin of 10 per cent is added to the total cost in order to determine the selling price.

The apportionment of the works' indirect overheads can be made on the following bases:

- Supervision: actual.
- Power: output.
- Depreciation: value of plant.
- Canteen expenses: numbers of employees.
- Maintenance: value of buildings.
- Rent and rates: area occupied.

  It should be stressed that the choice of the basis of apportionment is entirely subjective and other bases could be selected. However, the effect of different choices will affect the allocation of overheads, and ultimately the overhead recovery rates. The cautious accountant will always check to ensure that any possible differences, due to the application of different choices of allocation bases, are not significant.

The salaries have been apportioned in accordance with the time spent in the various departments. Power has been allocated on the basis of output, with department X being given a notional usage the same as department C.

Table 8.6 Overhead allocation sheet

	Department					
£000	A	B	C	X	Y	Z
Supervision	9	6	15		15	15
Power	18	18	12	12		
Depreciation	2	2	3.6	0.4	1	1
Canteen expenses	4	3	2	3	1	1
Maintenance	8	1.2	16	2	0.8	2
Rent and rates	6	6	4	2	1	1
Totals	47	36.2	52.6	19.4	18.8	20

Table 8.7 Reapportionment of service departments

£000	Department					
	A	B	C	X	Y	Z
Totals	47	36.2	52.6	19.4	18.8	20
Dept. Y	3.76	3.76	3.76	3.76	(18.8)	3.76
Dept. X	23.16			(23.16)		
Dept. Z	5.94	5.94	11.88			(23.76)
Totals	79.86	45.90	68.24			

Depreciation has been apportioned on the basis of the cost of the plant used by the departments and canteen expenses on the basis of numbers employed. Maintenance has been apportioned in relation to the value of the buildings occupied by the departments and rent and rates on the basis of the area occupied. These latter two items could well have been apportioned on the same basis, or the choices reversed. This is an example of the subjective nature of apportionment.

The reapportionment of the service departments' indirect overheads is illustrated in Table 8.7. Department Y is reapportioned first as this department services all other departments and, therefore, its costs will form part of the total costs of the other two service departments. Then the totals of the remaining service departments can be allocated.

The next stage is to calculate the recovery rates for the three production departments on the bases indicated.

Overhead recovery in department A is to be made on the basis of a plusage to material cost. The factors are as follows:

	£000
Budgeted material cost	400
Overheads department A, say	80
Recovery rate	20%

The recovery in department B is to be made on the basis of labour cost. The calculation is:

	£000
Budgeted labour cost	50
Overheads department B, say	46
Recovery rate	90%

Finally, the recovery of overheads for department C is to be made on the basis of a machine hour rate. The relevant factors are:

Budgeted machine hours	10,000
Overheads department C, say	£68,000
Machine hour rate	£6.80

It is also necessary to calculate the rates at which both administration, and selling and distribution, will be recovered to works cost and cost of production respectively. These are calculated as follows:

Administration overheads

	£000
Budgeted material cost	400
Budgeted labour cost	50
Budgeted prime cost	450
Budgeted works overheads	194
Budgeted works cost	644
Budgeted administration cost	70
Recovery rate, say	11%

Selling and distribution overheads

	£000
Budgeted works cost (above)	644
Budgeted administration cost	70
Budgeted cost of production	714
Budgeted selling and distribution cost	45
Recovery rate, say	6%

When the recovery rates have been calculated for the ensuing year they can then be applied for both estimating purposes and for cost control purposes. (This latter aspect is dealt with in Chapter 12.) An estimate of the selling price can now be prepared in respect of the data previously detailed. The overheads in respect of department A are the material cost multiplied by the recovery rate of 20 per cent, for department B the multiplication of the labour cost by the recovery rate of 90 per cent, and for department C the rate of £6.80 per hour applied to the estimated machine hours. Then a further addition is made in respect of administration overheads of 11 per cent of the works cost and to obtain the total cost an addition of 6 per cent of the cost of production in respect of selling and distribution overheads. An addition is then made in respect of profit, to arrive at the estimated selling price.

It should be noted that of the total cost of £1,827, only £1,150, or 63 per cent, is direct cost. The remainder represents the allocation of indirect costs. Thus the choice of bases for the process of allocation and apportionment is a significant element in the determination of individual product

Table 8.8 Estimate of selling price

		£
Direct material		1,000
Direct labour		150
Prime cost		1,150
overheads:		
Dept. A	200	
Dept. B	135	
Dept. C	68	403
Works cost		1,553
Administration cost		171
Cost of production		1,724
Selling and distribution cost		103
Total cost		1,827
Add profit (10% on total cost)		183
Estimated selling price		2,010

costs. The total amount of indirect costs will not be affected by this process – only the amounts that are 'shared out' between the individual products. Thus different bases may result in individual product costs being higher or lower, with the implied consequences for both profitability and market competitiveness.

In the event that the estimate becomes an order, then the estimated profit will only be made if all the elements in the estimate – material usage, labour hours and machine hours utilised, and costs arising at budgeted levels – are controlled at the estimated levels.

CONCLUSIONS

The determination of individual product costs, by whatever method, is a matter of primary importance to efficient and profitable management. By its very nature, it is a process that requires a detailed analysis of both the organisational structure of the firm and of the production methods adopted within that structure. In order to obtain data that are of sufficient accuracy for control purposes it is a process that cannot be abridged – any attempt to do so will result in data that are of inferior quality and utility.

The purpose of costing is to provide information for the managerial control of costs and for making crucial decisions. Consider the costing aspects of the business, with particular reference to the points set out below.

KEY LEARNING POINTS

The determination of product costs involves the following stages:

- **The classification of costs.**
- **Identification of indirect overheads by function.**
- **Allocation and apportionment of indirect costs.**
- **Reallocation of service department indirect costs.**
- **Selection and calculation of departmental overhead recovery rates.**
- **Compilation of individual job costs.**
- **Process costs.**
- **Control of overhead costs.**

CASE STUDY

1 Prepare an overhead allocation sheet for the year to 31 December 19X3, giving due regard to the departments of the firm and to the need for Peter French to be able to determine the costs of operating his various activities.

Approximately one-third of the cost of the craftsmen and assistants is booked to customers' jobs.

2 Calculate an appropriate overhead recovery rate for the manufacturing department.

3 Calculate the selling price of the following models if 10 per cent is added to total cost as a profit margin:

Balmoral	– direct material costs	£250.00
	– direct labour hours	20
Sandringham	– direct material costs	£300.00
	– direct labour hours	25

The direct labour hour cost is £4.00, and 7,000 hours are budgeted for the year.

Chapter 9

Cost behaviour

INTRODUCTION

It is generally appreciated that when the output of a firm rises, by say, 10 per cent, the costs do not rise by the same proportion, but will rise by a lesser percentage. Conversely, when output falls then the reduction in costs is generally less than the percentage fall in output. The reason for this is a result of the manner in which costs behave.

TYPES OF COST

There are two types of cost:

- **Variable (direct) costs**   These vary proportionately with variations in the output of the firm. In other words, a 10 per cent increase in output produces a 10 per cent increase in variable costs. Examples would be the direct material cost or the direct labour cost of a product. The concept of labour as a variable cost is one that must be treated with reservation, as there is a great deal of evidence that it is more fixed than variable.
- **Fixed (time-based) costs**   These costs arise as a result of the passage of time – e.g. salaries, rent, rates, etc., and do not vary as output rises or falls but remain at one level as their incidence is influenced by the size and the policies of the firm.

There is a third category of cost – semi-variable cost – that is probably more prevalent, across the accounting definitions of cost, than either of the other two, and these are those categories of cost that are influenced, to a greater or lesser extent by both the variable and fixed characteristics. A simple example is a salesman's salary that comprises an element of basic salary (fixed) and an element of commission (variable) in the total. Another example is of the power costs in a foundry, where the incidence of cost would be influenced by the level of activity (variable) and the sliding scale of charges for consumption made by the electricity company (fixed).

In both cases the cost can be segregated into its variable and fixed components by one of a number of methods, ranging from a simple 'high–low' approach, to the use of regression analysis. (See appendix on p. 122.) Thus for the purposes of understanding the behaviour of cost it can be assumed with confidence that there are just two categories of cost.

Difficulty will be experienced if an attempt is made to segregate conventional accounting classifications of cost into any sort of behavioural characteristic. It must be appreciated that the majority of costs will be semi-variable and that it is necessary to determine the totals of both fixed and variable costs and to resist the temptation to classify their respective components by accounting classification, e.g. telephone or heating and lighting.

COST, REVENUE, VOLUME RELATIONSHIPS

The behaviour of cost can best be appreciated by considering the manner in which the two costs behave in relation to output, as depicted in Figures 9.1–9.3. The horizontal axes represents output starting at the left at zero and increasing as the line progresses to the right. The vertical axes represents value, staring at zero at the base and increasing as the line progresses upwards. In Figure 9.1 the line F_1–F_2 represents the fixed costs, which appear as a straight line parallel to the output line. The line V_1–V_2 in Figure 9.2 represents the variable costs, and increases in a linear relationship to increases in output. It is at zero when output is at zero and as output increases, so does the total variable cost by the variable cost of each unit.

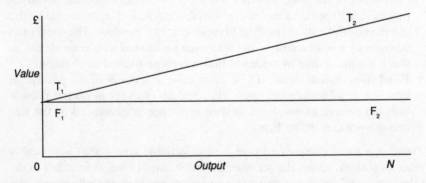

Figure 9.1 Fixed costs and total costs

Given that there are only two types of cost it follows logically that if these are added together then the total will represent the total cost of the firm at each level of output. This can be done either by 'adding' the variable cost line on to the fixed cost line making the line T_1–T_2 (see

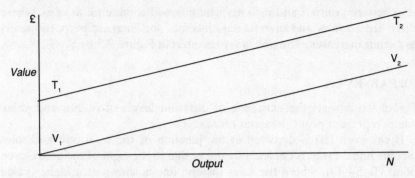

Figure 9.2 Variable costs and total costs

Figure 9.2) the total cost line as in Figure 9.1 or by 'adding' the fixed cost parallelogram (see Figure 9.1) on to the variable cost line, making the line F_1–F_2 (see Figure 9.1) the total cost line (as in Figure 9.2). Either method produces exactly the same line for total cost.

Close observation of the total cost line will reveal a fundamental truth about cost behaviour: all increases of total cost are increases of variable cost.

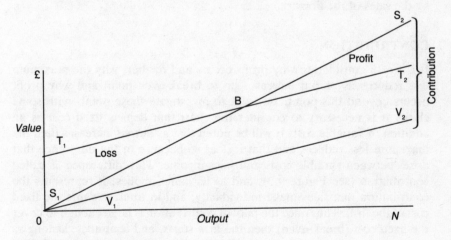

Figure 9.3 Break-even chart

It must be added that the rule needs qualifying: 'all other things remaining equal'. Nonetheless, it is a very valuable rule that is extremely useful for both cost analysis and decision-making purposes.

A further modification can now be made to the chart in respect of sales income. As with the variable costs, this line will reflect the linear relationship between output and income. The line will commence at zero, where there are no sales and therefore no income, and increase proportionately as output increases. The line is represented in Figure 9.3 by S_1–S_2.

BREAK-EVEN

Figure 9.3 reveals the existence of different levels of output and value which represent profit, loss and break-even.

Break-even (B) is depicted at the junction of the total cost and sales income lines. Profit is depicted by the wedge to the right of the break-even point (B–S_2–T_2), where the sales income line is shown at a higher value than the total cost line, and loss is depicted to the left of this point where the total costs are shown at a higher value than the sales income (B–S_1–T_1).

Careful observation of the chart will reveal that the maximum loss shown is equal to the fixed costs.

This is the second fundamental truth about cost behaviour revealed by the break-even chart. Intrinsic to the nature of fixed cost, from the point of view of profit maximisation, is the fact that any item of fixed cost, be it the chairman's salary or the rent of the premises, is totally non-productive in terms of earning profit, and must be financed from the revenues generated by the sales of the firm.

CONTRIBUTION

It is worth considering why profit occurs and further, why the maximum loss reduces as output increases up to break-even point and why profit occurs beyond this point. In order to investigate these points with some clarity it is necessary to consider the chart that depicts fixed cost as an addition to variable cost. It will be noted that as output increases then the maximum loss reduces and that it does so because of the difference that arises between variable costs and sales income. This 'difference' is called contribution (see Figure 9.3), and as its name implies, it represents the contribution that sales make individually, and in total, towards the fixed cost of the firm. Thus once the pool of contribution is large enough to cover the fixed cost (break-even) then the firm starts, and continues, as long as output increases, to make profit. This leads logically to the third fundamental truth about cost behaviour:

Profit is contribution; specifically, it is contribution on all units of output above break-even point.

These points can be illustrated by the simple example of a firm which makes and sells one product at £10.00. The variable costs are £5.00 per unit and the firm's fixed costs are £5,000.00. The profit (loss) at three levels of

Table 9.1 Illustration of the rules of cost behaviour

Output (units)	500 £	1,000 £	1,500 £
Sales (£10.00 each)	5,000	10,000	15,000
Variable costs (£5.00 per unit)	2,500	5,000	7,500
Contribution (£5.00 per unit)	2,500	5,000	7,500
Less fixed cost	5,000	5,000	5,000
Profit (loss)	(2,500)	–	2,500

output are given in Table 9.1. Thus the operation of the three fundamental rules can be observed:

- All increases in total cost are increases of variable cost – note the totals of the variable and fixed costs at the three levels shown and that the increase is due solely to the increase in the variable cost.
- The maximum loss is equal to the fixed costs. Consider the situation at zero output where there would be no sales income, no variable cost and the fixed cost would comprise the loss.
- That profit is contribution, specifically contribution on all units of output above break-even point. The break-even point is at 1,000 units and the profit at 1,500 units of output is £2,500, which is equal to the contribution at 500 units of output. 1,500 units of output is 500 units above break-even point.

Two further points emerge from the above illustration:

1 Contribution is the reciprocal of variable costs. Thus if variable costs represent 50 per cent of sales then contribution must also represent 50 per cent; or if variable costs represent 70 per cent of sales, then contribution will represent 30 per cent of sales.
2 Break-even point (B) is obtained by dividing fixed costs (F) by the contribution per unit (C):

$$B = F / C$$

In the above example, break-even point is:

$$£5,000/5.00 = 1,000 \text{ units}$$

LIMITATIONS OF BREAK-EVEN CHARTS

Unfortunately the analysis described thus is far too simplistic for even the most basic of firm, and it is necessary to consider the limitations of break-even charts (and of break-even analysis) before proceeding further.

Point in time

The main limitation of the break-even chart is that it represents the position at a single point in time. Any variations to the values of the variables used in its construction will necessitate a redrafting. Provided that this limitation is recognised, it is not an insurmountable obstacle to the chart's utilisation for decision-making.

Assumptions of linearity

The assumption that costs can be predicted over significant ranges of output is a major error. A moment's reflection will give rise to the realisation that with increasing levels of output, costs per unit will begin to fall – first from economies of scale, and second from the increasing benefits of both productivity and from the use of technology. Thus the variable cost line will not continue at the same angle as output increases, but will begin to decline as the range increases. Additionally, fixed cost will not continue at the same level over ranges of output but, as output increases, will also increase as additional elements of fixed cost are required to service the extra volumes of output. These increases will include the costs of extra capacity, such as additional administration, selling and distribution costs, all of which will include a large element of fixed cost. This increase can be represented as a series of 'steps' on the break-even chart, at selected points on the range, but even this is a simplification of the reality of the situation where fixed costs will continue to rise as output rises, albeit at a lower rate than for variable costs. Over wide measures of the output range there is evidence that fixed costs behave in roughly the same manner as variable costs.

Assumptions of product mix

The firm that produces and markets one product is the exception rather than the rule – even the smallest of firms will market a range of products, all of which will have their own unique selling price/contribution relationship. In order to construct a break-even chart it is necessary to assume that a constant mix will prevail – an assumption that experience indicates to be the exception rather than the rule. It can, however, be a useful 'short-hand' towards the preparation of a break-even chart and very often, in practice, an assumption that is supportable can be made and the chart used for decisions.

Problems of homogeneity of product output

Another major drawback to the construction of break-even charts is the necessity to produce a measure of output that equates one product with another, so that the previously mentioned assumption can be made. It is too simplistic to use the common denominator of selling prices, because this assumes that each £'s worth of sales equates to the equivalent use of productive capacity, and it is this latter factor that generates the costs. In order to overcome this problem it is necessary to define all products by a common denominator. In the engineering industry this might be achieved by the use of a measure of input i.e. standard hours, as a measure of the homogeneity of output. Each case will need to be carefully considered on its merits in the light of individual circumstances.

A moment's consideration of a simple firm, such as a newsagent's shop, will identify the crucial nature of this problem. There will be four broad product categories – papers, tobacco, confectionery and other goods – within each of which there will be a range of products, all of which will have their own unique sale/contribution ratio. It is not too fanciful to suggest that the total product range will run into hundreds. Yet in order to produce a break-even chart for the business it is necessary to assume a constant product mix. It can be done, and certainly minor variations will not affect the utility of the chart (for the purpose of making decisions) but any such decisions must take into account this constraint.

Relevant range

Notwithstanding the above-mentioned constraints, the break-even chart remains a very useful aid for making decisions. It has been suggested that its greatest utility is the benefit that is derived from determining the value of the variables necessary for its construction in any given situation. Certainly it is indisputable that that the management of any firm that undertakes such a task will have a very clear view of a number of important factors, pertinent to that firm, namely, the variable costs of each product, its contribution, the optimal product mix and the fixed costs at the current level of activity. It is a very short step to determine the changes that will occur as output moves (marginally) above or below the current level of activity. Thus as a generalisation it can be concluded that break-even charts have a high degree of utility between fairly limited ranges of output – the relevant range. The precise extent of this range will differ from firm to firm, being dependent on factors such as size, range of products, complexity of manufacturing processes etc.

BREAK-EVEN ANALYSIS

Alternative presentation

The construction of a break-even chart and its use for decision-making is somewhat complicated by its presentation. The significant factors are the level of contribution, at various stages of output, and the level of fixed costs. The chart can be constructed by using these two elements. In this presentation the vertical axis is used to measure profit and loss, with break-even being represented by zero on this scale, and output is measured on the horizontal axis. Losses are measured below the horizontal axis, with fixed costs representing the maximum loss at zero output. The contribution per unit is then measured for each unit of output (assuming a constant product mix), with the result that the loss reduces as output increases, until break-even occurs where the contribution line crosses the output line. Thereafter the contribution on each unit of output represents profit, which is plotted above the output line.

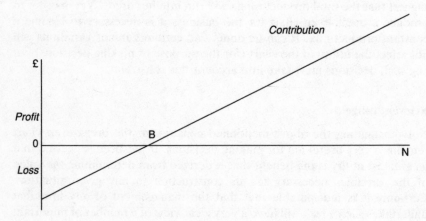

Figure 9.4 Profit–volume graph

This presentation – the profit–volume graph – has the merit of drawing attention to the salient points of profit, break-even and loss relative to various levels of output. A pertinent, and telling, point can be made when the horizontal axis is converted into a time-scale, i.e. a month or a year. Consider the case of the average supermarket, which has a profit of 4.9 per cent on sales (cited in *The Economist*, 23 February 1991). When this is transferred to the output scale it shows that break-even (on an annual basis) occurs some 2.6 weeks before the end of the financial year! Such a presentation reveals the transient nature of profit. The annual fixed costs take 49.4 weeks of the year (including holidays) to be covered.

Table 9.2 Product mix

Product	Mix	Contribution per unit
A	70%	£15.00
B	20%	£30.00
C	10%	£50.00
Average contribution 21.50		

Contribution/sales ratio

The relevant contribution measure that should be utilised is the average contribution of the sales mix. This can be illustrated as shown in Table 9.2. Clearly, management's marketing strategies will be aimed at increasing the proportion of the mix for products B and C, which will be resisted by the consumer because of their relatively higher selling prices (the lower rate of contribution on product A indicating its lower selling price and, therefore, its increased price competitiveness).

In the event that the sales mix changes, then the break-even chart, or profit/volume graph, must be redrafted to reflect the changed circumstances.

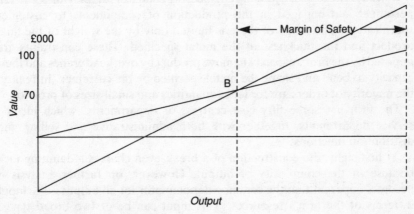

Figure 9.5 Margin of safety

Margin of safety

Once a break-even chart has been constructed for any given situation, one of the most pertinent measures will be the current level of sales. The difference between this level of output and the break-even point is known as the margin of safety. Clearly this is a measurement that is of extreme importance to management, in that the greater the margin of safety, the greater the fall in sales (and therefore both contribution and profit) before the firm starts incurring losses. In Figure 9.5, sales are at £100,000 and the break-even point is £70,000. The margin of safety is 30 per cent, the difference between the current level of output and the break-even point. If sales fall to £80,000 then the margin of safety will also fall, in this case to 12.5 per cent; conversely, if the sales increase then the margin of safety also increases. Nonetheless, the importance of the measurement for management control can be appreciated.

ILLUSTRATION

One of the major problems with break-even analysis in practice is the fact that virtually all firms make and/or sell more than one product. Thus in the construction of a break-even chart, an assumption regarding product mix needs to be made, or a subjective apportionment of fixed cost needs to be made, in order to produce break-even analyses for each product or product group. The consequence of this dilemma is that, at best, only approximations of break-even points can be calculated. Within these constraints the management of a firm need to reduce the variables in the equation to the simplest level possible so that the analysis can be used to extrapolate alternative scenarios for decision-making purposes. (See Chapter 10.)

Consider the case of a jobbing engineering company, employing some 120 personnel and engaged in the production of components to customer specification. The range of these is limited only by the weight of the final product and the thickness of the metal specified. These constraints are imposed by the firm's capacity to move product by overhead cranes and their capacity to bend and shape the metal specified by the customer. In reality, the majority of orders are for large quantities and small sizes of product.

The firm has some fifty cost centres, or departments, which include service departments, together with both administrative and selling and distribution functions.

At first sight, the construction of a break-even chart is a daunting task because of the complexity of output. However, on further analysis it becomes apparent that the common denominator for all output is the input in terms of the firm's resources. This input can be of two broad types: specialised man hours, of a variety of skills, and machine hours, again of a variety of types. The problem was overcome by defining all output in terms of its production value – in this case, a hybrid hour. In practice it did not matter whether or not an order was for a large, complex single item, or for a large quantity of small easily produced products; in both cases the output measure was the same – the number of 'hours' required for production.

Thus the horizontal axis of the chart could now be measured in terms of a common quantity. The level of fixed costs was determined by regression analysis (see the appendix to this chapter), as was the variable cost per 'hour'. These values were calculated from the annual budgets and carefully checked on a monthly basis using annual moving averages to ensure that they remained accurate to an acceptable level.

The firm continued to estimate all enquiries using the process outlined in Chapter 8. They now also calculated the contribution from each enquiry. This was compared with the level of demand, and pragmatic decisions could be made regarding the relative selling price that could be offered in respect of particular orders.

The following is an illustration of this process:

		£000
Annual costs:		
Payroll		1,500
Other		3,000
Fixed cost per annum		4,000
Variable cost per 'hour'	£5.00	
Annual 'hours'	100,000	
Target selling price per 'hour'	£50.00	

The break-even point can be calculated as:

Contribution per 'hour'	(£50 – £5)	£45.00
Fixed costs per annum		£4,000,000

Break-even (£4.0m./£45), say 89,000 'hours'

Thus the margin of safety at maximum capacity was only 11 per cent.

Given the implication of such a low margin of safety, at maximum capacity, it was essential that all enquiries were competitively priced. The firm was able to utilise their knowledge of contribution per 'hour' to ensure that all quotations incorporated a satisfactory margin.

CONCLUSIONS

Current trends are towards higher levels of fixed costs for all types of businesses, due mainly to increased levels of technology. This investment is represented in two ways, first by the annual depreciation charge on the equipment, and second by the cost associated with such investments in terms of salaries, maintenance and higher labour costs which reflect an increasing specialisation. The consequence of such a trend is that break-even points, even among smaller concerns, are at higher levels of capacity, with a consequent reduction in the margin of safety at normal levels of activity. This trend has been accelerating over the past two decades or so and there is no evidence that it will abate.

The inevitable result of such a situation is that management's control of operational costs needs to become more accurate. One aspect of this control is a clear understanding of the factors that contribute to the profitability of current operations.

These include:

- Identification of the variable cost of each product, and of their contribution at differing selling prices.
- A constant analysis of the sales mix of individual product levels of output.
- Identification of fixed costs, together with their constant monitoring to eliminate wasteful expenditure.

KEY LEARNING POINTS

- **All costs can be analysed into fixed and variable categories.**
- **All increases in total costs (excluding price changes) are increases of variable costs, reflecting increases or decreases in output.**
- **The maximum loss that a firm can incur is equal to its fixed costs.**
- **The difference between selling price and variable cost is the contribution.**
- **Profit is contribution – specifically, it is the contribution on all units of output above break-even point.**

CASE STUDY

Calculate the break-even point (in terms of sales) for Peter French in respect of each of the years 19X0, 19X1 and 19X2, and comment on the position revealed by the analysis.

Calculate the margin of safety in each of the three years.

APPENDIX: SEMI-VARIABLE COSTS

The analysis of semi-variable costs can be made in three different ways:

- by observation;
- by finding the 'line of best fit';
- by calculation using regression analysis.

Observation

This is usually known as the 'high–low' method and involves comparing total costs and levels of output in successive periods as illustrated in Table 9.3, the difference being the level of variable costs. Division of the difference in the level of output into the difference in the level of total costs gives the variable costs per unit. Obviously it can only be applied in respect of homogeneity of product output. This is a simple approach that, at best, will give an indication of the variable element of cost.

Table 9.3 High–low method of calculating variable costs

	Month 1	Month 2	Difference
Output	1,200	1,400	+ 200
Total costs	£26,400	£29,400	+ £3,000

Variable costs per unit = (£3,000/200) = £15.00

Table 9.4 Cost and output data

	Output (tonnes)	Costs
Month 1	1,000	£10,000
Month 2	1,400	12,000
Month 3	1,200	16,000
Month 4	1,800	14,000
Month 5	1,500	18,000
Month 6	1,300	11,000
Month 7	1,600	14,000
Month 8	1,500	16,000
Month 9	1,000	10,000
Month 10	1,800	12,000
Month 11	1,400	13,000
Month 12	1,200	11,000
Totals	16,700	£157,000

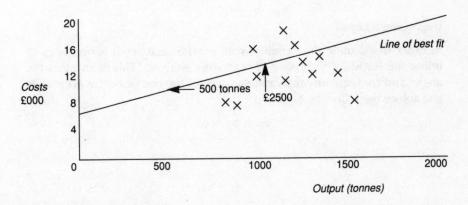

Figure 9.6 Line of best fit

Line of best fit

This is a more sophisticated approach, that will give a reasonably accurate determination of the variable element of costs. It involves the construction of a break-even chart on which the costs are plotted for (preferably) a twelve-month period. That is to say that twelve plots are made of consecutive monthly costs against the levels of output for those months. Consider Table 9.4, which is an illustration of a twelve-month period, where the costs in question are electricity costs in a foundry and the output is the tonnage produced. The 'line of best fit' is found by judging the angle at which a line will best bisect the plots entered on the graph (Figure 9.6). The variable cost is calculated by measuring the increase in costs, as represented by the angle of the line, against the increase in output for the same range, and by dividing the cost increase by the increase in output. The fixed costs are the amount where the line of best fit crosses the vertical axis. In effect, the line of best-fit is the total cost line in a break-even chart.

In the illustration, the increase in costs is £2,500 for an increase of 500 tonnes. Thus the variable cost per tonne is £5.00. One of the rules of cost behaviour is that all increases in total cost are increases of variable cost. The line bisects the vertical axis at £6,000, which is the level of fixed costs per month. A check on the data reveals that, from these calculations, the total costs are £155,500, which is a sufficiently accurate estimation.

Although the resultant value for variable cost is accurate, the main problem lies in the individual's perception of the angle of the line; clearly, were this to be different then the resultant costs would also vary. A partial solution to this problem in practice is to use the twelve-month sample as a moving average. That is, to make the calculation each month and to add the current month while deleting the same month from the previous year, i.e the oldest in the sample. The results should be similar on a month-to-month basis, any marginal changes being the result of price changes.

Regression analysis

In order to calculate the variables with precise accuracy it is necessary to utilise the statistical technique of regression analysis. This determines the angle, and consequently the variable costs, of the line of best fit accurately and solves the following equation:

$$ax + by = tc$$

where: a = variable cost per unit
        x = total output for the period
        b = fixed costs per month
        y = number of months in the sample
and tc = total costs

Illustrating this technique would be beyond the scope of this book; reference can be made to any basic statistics textbook for further information.

Chapter 10

Costs for decisions

INTRODUCTION

Costs that are used for short-term decisions must be those that are pertinent to the decision; those that do not affect the decision in question should be excluded.

Marginal costs are applied, over time, to a large number of problems, and absorption costs involve decisions on the basis of allocated and apportioned overheads. In neither case do such costs identify the particular costs that are pertinent to any specific decision, because both criteria either involve costs that are allocated (absorption costs) or may exclude costs that are pertinent, such as fixed costs in the case of marginal costs.

Managers may face difficulties in identification of the particular costs pertinent to a decision circumstance, due to the construction of accounting reports which, generally, do not segregate the appropriate costs to facilitate decisions.

For the purposes of short-term decision making, costs should be classified as follows:

- **Relevant costs**   Those costs that are pertinent to a decision. It follows that such costs must also be future costs, as only these can be affected by a decision. These costs are also defined as differential, or incremental costs.
- **Sunk costs**   Any cost which has already been incurred and which cannot therefore be affected by the decision.
- **Opportunity costs**   These represent the benefits forgone by a particular decision and must therefore be considered as part of the costs of making that decision. The concept is an economic one and can be illustrated by the decision to purchase an article. The alternative option (which always exists) is not to make the purchase, and the interest forgone if the purchase is made must be considered as part of the cost. This has important implications for management in evaluating short-term decisions.

This concept should not be confused with that of discounting, utilised for purposes of investment appraisal, which takes into account the time value of money; such decisions are essentially long-term.

RELEVANT COSTS

Consider Table 10.1, which is an example concerning the costs of running a car with an annual mileage of 10,000 miles. After a change of employment the car's owner finds that he has an additional journey of forty miles per day and that he can either use his car or travel by public transport at a cost of £4.00 per day, both of which are equally convenient. The decision can be evaluated by considering the relevant or differential costs for the additional mileage, as shown in Table 10.2.

Table 10.1 Total costs per mile

Costs	pence per mile
Depreciation (£1,500 p.a.)	15.0
Maintenance (£60 every 5,000 miles)	0.6
Maintenance (£120 every 10,000 miles)	1.2
Tyres (£100 every 20,000 miles)	0.5
Licence & insurance (£300 p.a.)	3.0
Petrol & oil (£2.20 p.g. @ 35 mpg.)	6.3
Annual interest on £6,000 purchase price (£720 p.a.)	7.2
Total cost per mile	33.8

Table 10.2 Relevant costs per mile

	pence per mile
Maintenance – 5,000 mile service	0.6
Maintenance – 10,000 mile service	1.2
Tyres	0.5
Petrol & oil	6.3
Total relevant cost per mile	8.6
Total differential cost per trip	£3.44

It should be noted that all sunk costs (i.e. those that cannot be affected by the decision) have been excluded – only those costs that will arise as a result of the decision are relevant to that decision.

The car should be used, purely on the basis of financial considerations. There may, however, be other (non-financial) factors that could affect such a decision, and some consideration should be given to these.

Managers are constantly called upon to make similar types of decision in the context of their daily responsibilities and an example could be the decision as to which of two machines should be used for a particular order. Details of the operating costs of the two machines are provided in Table 10.3. Table 10.4 shows calculation of the hourly operating rates. An order is received (job ABC) for 300 units of output, which can be produced on machine A at 30 units per hour or on machine B at 50 units per hour. The material cost of the job is £100.00. The comparative machine hour rates, using the total (absorption) cost approach, are shown in Table 10.5. The material costs are irrelevant to the decision, as they are the same for both alternatives.

According to the absorption approach the firm will utilise machine A to undertake the job. However, utilising a differential cost approach (Table 10.6), sunk costs will be excluded. These are those that cannot be affected by the decision and are, in this case, the fixed costs which will arise whether or not the job is undertaken. According to the differential approach, the firm is indifferent to the use of either machine, as the incremental costs are the same. It must be stated, however, that in the majority of cases that the manager would adopt the absorption approach as this would be based on the data supplied to him for decision purposes by the firm's accounting department.

OPPORTUNITY COSTS

These have previously been defined as the cost of the forgone next-best alternative, and as a concept that has its roots in economic theory. Nonetheless it is of paramount importance in the context of decision-making that the benefits that are lost due to making a particular decision are considered as part of the total cost of that decision. Consider the following examples.

Example 1

There are three alternatives, which will increase profit by £10,000, £6,000 and £3,000 respectively. If the first is not accepted, its opportunity cost is £4,000 (i.e. £10,000 − £6,000) and this must be considered as a cost of the second alternative. Admittedly it is difficult to conceive of circumstances in which the first would not be accepted.

Example 2

Stock is held that cost £500; its scrap value is £50. If this is used for producing X and nothing else, the material cost of X is £50 because the opportunity cost is that of the best alternative, which is to scrap the material. An opportunity arises where the material can be used for an order of £600.00, but which will incur processing costs of £200.00.

Table 10.3 Machine operating costs

	Machine A (1 operator)	Machine B (2 operators)
Annual operating hours	2,000	1,800
Hourly rate (operators)	£3.00	£3.00
Variable operating cost per machine hour	£1.65	£1.75
Fixed operating costs per annum	£4,000	£7,200

Table 10.4 Calculation of hourly operating rates

	Machine A	Machine B
Operators' wages	£3.00	£6.00
Variable costs	1.65	1.75
Total variable costs	4.65	7.75
Fixed costs	2.00	4.00
Total hourly cost	£6.65	£11.75

Table 10.5 Absorption costs

	Machine A	Machine B
Units per hour	30	50
Hours required	10	6
Cost per hour	£6.65	£11.75
Total cost of job ABC	£66.50	£70.50

Table 10.6 Relevant costs

Machine A	10 hours @ £4.65	£46.50
Machine B	6 hours @ £7.75	£46.50

Table 10.7 Profit statement – absorption cost approach

Sale price		£600
Material costs	£500	
Processing costs	£200	£700
Loss		£100

Table 10.8 Profit statement – relevant cost approach

Sale price		£600
Material cost		
(opportunity cost)	£ 50	
Processing costs	200	250
Profit		£350

Under the absorption approach, the evaluation would be as shown in Table 10.7. Utilising this approach the opportunity would be rejected. However, if the differential (or opportunity) cost approach is adopted, then a different picture emerges. Clearly, if the order is accepted then the firm will be better off by £350 as a result, because the 'cost' of the material is only £50, which would be the return on the alternative course of action to accepting the order. The other alternative, which always exists, is to do nothing. However, this would involve the firm in a loss of £500 which is the cost of the material, for which there is no other use. If there is a case for considering that a use may arise in the future, then this must be evaluated and compared with the existing set of alternatives. It has been pointed out previously that profit is opinion, whereas cash is fact, and this point is very pertinent when making decisions. A practical example of the application of opportunity costs is the widespread practice, in the retail trade, of having seasonal sales. These are not only used to attract additional custom but are also used for the purpose of converting unsold stock into cash so that the proceeds can be used for further purchasing of additional stock for resale.

The criteria for accurate decision-making can be summarised as:

- a precise picture of the alternatives available;
- an understanding of the different cost concepts;
- a flexible classification of accounting data to enable the relevant costs of the various alternatives to be identified.

Other common types of decisions are the addition or deletion of a product or division, and the decision to make or subcontract products or part of products.

ADDING OR DELETING A PRODUCT OR A DEPARTMENT

Once again, the costs and revenues concerned are the relevant ones, that is those that are directly concerned with the addition or deletion. Consider the following example of the deletion of a division in a firm which operates three divisions. The accounting reports are as shown in Table 10.9. It should be noted that the fixed costs have been allocated on a subjective basis. The implication from the report is that the closure of department C would increase net profitability by £20,000, which is the loss reported for that department. Table 10.10 shows the effect of such a decision. It will be noticed that far from increasing the profit by the amount of the loss of department C, profits have fallen. The amount of the fall is equal to the contribution provided by department C. The reason for the fall in profit is that the fixed costs have had to be allocated over the two remaining departments.

Table 10.9 Departmental profit statement (before closure)

£000	Total	Dept. A	Dept. B	Dept. C
Sales	600	400	150	50
Variable costs	395	300	75	20
Contribution	205	100	75	30
Fixed costs	150	50	50	50
Profit (loss)	55	50	25	(20)

Table 10.10 Departmental profit statement (after closure)

£000	Total	Dept. A	Dept. B
Sales	550	400	150
Variable costs	375	300	75
Contribution	175	100	75
Fixed costs	150	75	75
Profit (loss)	25	25	–

This illustration reinforces the previously mentioned rule that 'profit is contribution, specifically contribution on all units of output above break-even point'.

It may be that some of the fixed costs were specific to department C, in which case the report requires amendment to reflect this situation. The amended report also reflects the general principle that there is no point in indulging in arbitrary allocation of general fixed costs merely to attempt to identify the net profit position of either departments or products. Such an approach is untenable because of the arbitrary and subjective nature of the process of allocation and apportionment of indirect overheads.

Table 10.11 Departmental profit statement – marginal presentation

£000	Total	Dept. A	Dept. B	Dept. C
Sales	600	400	150	50
Variable costs	395	300	75	20
Contribution	205	100	75	30
Dept. fixed cost	50	20	20	10
Dept. profit	155	80	55	20
General fixed cost	100			
Profit (loss)	55			

A revised report identifying the departmental fixed costs and not allocating the general fixed costs would appear as in Table 10.11. Thus the state of the profit-earning capacity of the firm is revealed, and any decision regarding the closure of a department can be made in respect of the relevant values which, in this case, are the departmental profit. Any attempt to analyse this further will result in the use of erroneous information for the purpose of the decision.

The decision to add a product or department would be made using the same criteria. The relevant value will be the additional profit at departmental (or product) level before any attempt is made to allocate general indirect overheads. This profit level is the contribution earned by the additional department or product, less any specific fixed cost that arises from that activity.

MAKE OR BUY DECISIONS

A common decision that arises is one that concerns the available resources of the firm and whether to produce goods in-house or to subcontract the work. Again, the relevant costs are those that arise as a result of the decision and any that are not pertinent should be ignored. A number of other factors may complicate such decisions but, essentially, the financial considerations are quite clear. It may arise that a firm operates an in-house service, e.g. printing, and an instruction is issued that all work done by the service department is to be 'competitive', that is the cost to other divisions or departments must be at or lower than other commercially obtained quotations. The comparison of costs is not the total cost of the producing department but the relevant costs of the particular order. Any costs of the department that are sunk must be ignored.

Consider the following example where a department produces one

Table 10.12 Summary of departmental costs

	£000
Materials	100
Direct wages	200
Departmental salaries	50
Variable overheads	100
Allocated fixed costs	200
Depreciation	50
Total annual departmental costs	700

product and an external quotation is obtained to provide the product at £65.00 per unit. The annual cost for the production of 10,000 units are shown in Table 10.12. Superficially, it would appear that the internal cost is £70.00 per unit but the sunk costs, which are the allocated fixed costs, are £200,000 and these would continue to arise and the relevant cost per unit is only £50.00, which makes the external price uneconomic.

Should there have been output of a number of different products the calculation would have been more complex, in that the relevant costs of the particular products under review would need to be calculated and the comparison made with the externally obtained price against these costs. What would not be included in the equation would be any sunk cost that would remain to accrue to the firm in the event of production being subcontracted.

In the example given above of a one-product situation, had the consideration been to subcontract and to close the department then the approach would have been exactly the same, in that the relevant costs would have been those that would have been saved, in the long run, by subcontracting.

ABSORPTION VERSUS MARGINAL COSTS

The major advantage of the absorption approach to the determination of individual product costs over the marginal approach is that all the costs of the firm are considered. Where the marginal approach is adopted, the problem that arises is that although each product, job or service may make a contribution to fixed costs, the total of such contributions may be less than the total of the fixed costs, with the consequence of a net loss arising. However, it must also be recognised that the determination of the absorption cost, notwithstanding the subjective nature of the approach, essentially determines the cost, which reflects any inefficiencies of the firm. It is determined in relation to the firm's productive methods and capacity and does not reflect the market conditions. Under these circumstances the firm can only use the absorption cost as a measure of the profitability of supply, and not as a mechanism for determining the selling price. In other words, the market price is the important factor and the absorption cost measures whether or not the firm can supply the market at a profit margin.

Firms can use the marginal approach to consider special circumstances, or to price work under conditions of marginal under-utilisation of capacity. In such circumstances any contribution that is earned is a reduction of losses that are being incurred. It is worth remembering that profit is contribution on output above break-even point, and therefore contribution that reduces losses is also worthwhile contribution.

It is important that managers can distinguish the appropriate approach that is necessary under differing circumstances.

Table 10.13 Breakdown of product costs

Variable materials	£0.50
labour	0.80
overheads	0.30
Total variable cost	1.60
Fixed	0.90
Total cost	£2.50

Consider a situation where a firm produces one product which sells at £3.00. The cost breakdown per unit is shown in Table 10.13. The firm is operating at a profit and receives an enquiry from a very large potential customer which wishes to place an order for 20,000 units but will require a discount on normal selling price of 20 per cent. In order to complete such an order the firm will need to work overtime, which will increase the labour cost by 0.40p per unit. Should the order be accepted?

Table 10.14 Evaluation of order – absorption approach

Normal selling price		£3.00
Less quantity discount (20%)		0.60
Net selling price		£2.40
Less total cost	£2.50	
Add labour increase	0.40	2.90
Net loss per product		£0.50

Table 10.15 Evaluation of order – marginal approach

Net selling price		£2.40
Relevant (variable) costs	£1.60	
Add labour increase	0.40	2.00
Net contribution per product		£0.40

The initial evaluation utilising the absorption (total cost) approach is as shown in Table 10.14. The initial reaction is to reject the enquiry, as a loss will be incurred, but closer consideration of the relevant costs (the marginal approach) reveals a different picture. By accepting the order, the firm will gain £8,000 (20,000 at £0.40). It would not affect the decision had the firm been operating below capacity and making a loss, because acceptance of the order would have reduced those losses by the contribution earned.

ILLUSTRATION

One of the most difficult decisions is that to be taken in a new business to determine a selling price. It involves the ascertainment of both variable costs per unit and of the fixed costs per month. Additionally, consideration needs to be given to the level of profit that the selling price is to include. Failure to allow for an adequate return on the capital invested in the enterprise will result, ultimately, in inadequate levels of remuneration for the investors and inadequate levels of retention to finance future levels of activity. On the other hand, the settling of a selling price that is too high will result in loss of sales, with similar consequences. It cannot be stressed too strongly that, at the end of the day, it is the market that determines the selling price, and, while there are 'niches' within markets, the managers of firms need to understand the nature of their own particular 'niche' very clearly.

The following example illustrates the main points concerned with this problem but, in a practical situation, consideration will need to be given to the growth that is expected in the immediate future.

A college lecturer is made redundant and rather than seek alternative employment decides to establish a small business publishing a specialist quarterly journal of interest to lecturers in further and higher education. Prior to redundancy he circulates all colleges with details of his proposal and receives an encouraging response.

All contributors to the journal would be paid at the rate of £50 per page of approximately 800 words, and it is planned that each edition of the journal will contain twenty-five pages. He plans to write at least three-quarters of the pages himself, to provide an element of income.

In view of his limited resources he cannot afford to make any losses from his total initial capital of approximately £22,500.

The best printing quotation was obtained as follows:

To printing journal 25 pages –

    1,000 copies minimum @   £2,200.00
    1,000 copies run-on @   £ 250.00

Circulars, on A4-size paper, to be sent by post, could be produced at a cost of £50.00 per thousand and a sample survey showed that a response rate of 20 per cent could be expected to carefully placed circulars to specialist lecturers in colleges and universities. The cost of envelopes, postage and the clerical work in sending out circulars, or journals, would be £300.00 per thousand. Incidental administrative costs associated with each quarterly issue were estimated to be £150.

The market research had indicated that the price for the quarterly journal should be between £2.00 and £3.75 and he decided that the price should be kept as low as possible in view of the need for increased sales, and profits, in the future.

The problem to be resolved is twofold: first, what price to charge for the periodical and, second, how many issues to produce each quarter. Clearly one will affect the other. The more periodicals that are produced, the lower the selling price can be set in order to recoup the costs and provide an income. On the other hand, there is the need to sell all of the production in order to achieve this end; failure to do so will result in a shortfall of costs and, possibly, no income.

He estimates that he will require an income of approximately £12,000 per annum.

Two immediate problems to be resolved are:

1 In considering the first issue, which costs are fixed and which are variable with the number of journals printed?
2 What is the lowest price that can be charged for the journal that will ensure that a loss is not made on the initial capital of £22,500?

Table 10.16 assesses the fixed costs. The variable costs, per issue of 1,000 copies, are shown in Table 10.17. The selling price per copy can be calculated as shown in Table 10.18. A price of, say, £3.25 can be charged, or he can opt for £3.00 per copy and accept a slightly reduced income in the initial stages. His income requirements, as for any manager in a business, have been treated as a fixed cost.

Table 10.16 Summary of fixed costs per issue

Writer's fees	£1,250
Administration costs	150
Printing[a]	1,950
Total fixed costs	£3,350
Required income, say	3,000
Total	£6,350

[a]As the variable (run-on) cost per thousand is £250 then the 'fixed' (one-off) set-up cost must be £1,950

Table 10.17 Summary of variable costs per 1,000 journals

Printing		£ 250
Circulars:	printing	250
	distribution	1,500
Journals:	distribution	300
Total variable cost per thousand		£2,300

Table 10.18 Calculation of selling price

Capital available	£22,500
less fixed cost	6,350
Available for variable costs	£16,150
@ £2,300 per thousand =	7.02
Therefore 7,000 copies can be produced	
Selling price = £22,500 / 7,000 =	£3.20 per copy

CONCLUSIONS

Similar decisions to those considered above need to be made by managers in all firms, and not just at commencement. In particular, the selling price decision is one that needs to be constantly reviewed in the light of changing market conditions. The other types of decision that have been discussed are necessarily made on a regular basis by managers, and it is of critical importance that the correct criteria are used for evaluating these, which can be summarised as:

- A precise picture of the alternatives (to the decision to be made) that are available.
- A clear understanding of the different cost concepts that are relevant to particular decisions.

In order to be able to apply these different concepts a flexible classification of accounting data is required which provides information as to the level and behaviour of costs under differing circumstances. The challenge to the accounting profession is to provide such a methodology to their managerial colleagues.

KEY LEARNING POINTS

- **The costs to be utilised for short-term decisions are relevant costs. These are, by definition, future costs, as a decision cannot affect, or be affected by, costs that have already been incurred.**
- **Past costs are sunk costs and are irrelevant to decisions which can only affect the future.**
- **Consideration must be given to the opportunity costs of a decision, which are the benefits forgone from the next best alternative, if that decision is taken.**
- **Care must be exercised when determining the profitability of departments, or products, that this is not influenced by allocations of costs that will still occur regardless of the decision.**

CASE STUDY

Prepare a departmental profit statement for the year ending 31 December 19X2. Consider those overhead costs that are fixed but which can be attributed to a departmental operation, and consider those overhead costs that are general to the enterprise as a whole.

Calculate the product mix for each of the three years 19X0, 19X1 and 19X2. Identify the contribution from each activity and comment on the relative profitability of these, and on any changes that are apparent.

Consider a situation where there is a need to clear long-standing items of stock. What criteria should be applied to determine the selling price of these items?

Chapter 11

Planning

INTRODUCTION

Budgetary control is a technique that is concerned with planning a firm's activities in the short term, usually for one year ahead. It involves a searching examination of the firm's resources and aims to produce a coordinated and comprehensive plan for the firm's activities for the period that can be used to control those activities during that period in such a manner as to achieve optimal performance in the light of the economic environment during the period. Thus it is a technique that involves both planning and control. Given the individual characteristics of firms it is neither possible nor desirable to produce a specification for this technique that can be applied to all organisations, but a general statement of principles that can be adapted by each organisation to suit its own particular requirements can be provided.

A budget is a plan to measure and control future activities – it is a financial plan based on future objectives for a future period.

It is a coordinated estimate of future revenues and costs, working capital, cash requirements and investment programmes necessary to achieve those objectives, both short- and long-term, serving as a tool in assisting management to achieve those goals.

In order to do so, effective control is required; the budget represents a set of yardsticks and guidelines for controlling the internal operations of the business. The differences between the plan and the actual results highlight the need for action by management. These may involve a change in the mode of operation or an amendment to the plan, with any implications that may arise in terms of the future objectives.

The three main elements in the budgeting process are:

- objectives;
- planning;
- control.

There are important feedback effects, in that the control function may require amendments to both planning and objectives. It must be stressed that budgeting is not a mechanistic process – it is dynamic, and involves every member of the management in an organisation.

LONG-RANGE PLANNING

Budgetary control is a technique that can be adopted on its own, in the short term, to beneficial effect, but it can also represent the short-term commitment to the achievement of longer-term strategic objectives. Firms that utilise strategic planning to identify future objectives, and then ident-ify goals for the achievement of those objectives will, by the nature of the technique, have quantified targets of performance established for a num-ber of periods ahead. This process is a dynamic one, in that during each period the objectives are reviewed for a further year and thus the planning horizon is maintained at a constant level. The determination of that horizon will be different for individual firms, and both the size of the firm and the nature of the market will influence the choice. A multinational drug manufacturer may have a planning horizon of several years in order to accommodate the necessary research and development of products, whereas a small firm may have a planning horizon of just one year because it is much more reactive to changes in the market and planning for any longer period would be purely academic. The objectives of all firms must, however, be expressed in financial terms, because the rationale for their existence is to maximise shareholder wealth and it follows that the objec-tives will reflect this and will be represented by such measures as earnings per share or return on capital employed.

A budget is a detailed plan that identifies levels of performance for all aspects of an organisation to achieve the first of those series of goals. As Figure 11.1 clearly shows, the final outcome of the budget preparation must accord with the objectives detailed in the corporate plan. In the event that this is not so, then every aspect must be reappraised in order to ensure that no opportunity for improvement has been overlooked. It must be recognised that in the event of the corporate objectives not being achiev-able, then those objectives must themselves be subjected to a reappraisal. Such a process is a continuous one and it is unusual that such a situation should arise. Figure 11.1 shows the process of both planning and control and illustrates the factors that will influence the preparation of the budgets. The long-range objectives are a major influence, but clearly the predomi-nant factor will be the most recent performance as represented by the immediate past, as it is most unlikely, even in the most dynamic of firms, that circumstances in the immediate future, i.e. next year, will change dramatically. Other factors will be the incorporation in the budgets of any known changes in the firm's resources e.g. the addition of new plant or an

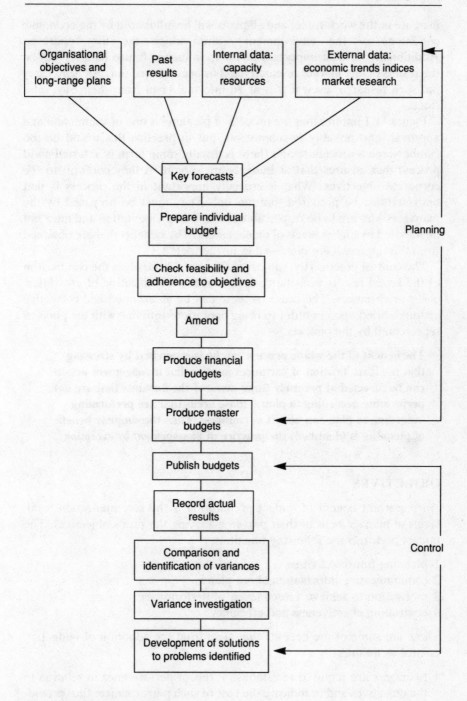

Figure 11.1 Budget process

increase in the work-force, and all plans will be influenced by the economic conditions of the environment within which the firm operates. Additionally, a most important factor to influence future budgets will be the results of any market research that has been carried out. All firms carry out such research, even if it is at an informal level from their own sales force.

Figure 11.1 implies that the process of planning is one of submission and approval, and possibly re-submission, but in practice this would be too cumbersome a procedure and there is usually some form of internal audit process that ensures that as budgets are submitted they conform to the corporate objectives. What is crucially important in the process is that budgets must be prepared 'bottom up'. They must be prepared by the managers who are to be responsible for their implementation and must not be imposed by higher levels of management. The benefits that are obtained from this approach are discussed in further detail.

The control process (the subject of Chapter 12) involves the comparison of the actual results with the budgets and the identification of any differences or variances. The cause of these can be ascertained and corrective action decided upon in order to bring operations into line with the plans as represented by the budgets.

The benefit of the whole process can be summarised by stressing that the identification of variances implies that management action can be directed at precisely those areas of the business that are not performing according to plan – those areas that are performing according to plan can be left to continue. Thus the singular benefit of planning is identified: the practice of *management by exception*.

OBJECTIVES

An important benefit of budget preparation is the communication to all levels of management of their part in achieving the firm's objectives. The budget performs the following functions:

1 planning future activities;
2 communicating information about plans;
3 motivation to achieve agreed levels of performance;
4 controlling effectiveness and efficiency.

These are some of the benefits that arise from the adoption of budgetary control techniques:

1 Managers are required to establish levels of performance in relation to the objectives and to indicate the cost of such performance, thus providing a benchmark against which actual performance can be assessed.

2 Effective planning requires the coordination of different activities within an organisation. For example, the purchasing function is obliged to consider production requirements, inventory policy and the cash resources necessary to fulfil obligations to suppliers. It does therefore compel goal congruence.

3 Management is obliged to give consideration to future activities, thus directing attention to pertinent aspects of efficiency and economy.

4 Organisation is improved as the various activities necessary to the attainment of the objectives have been coordinated and identified as the responsibility of specific managers. Thus each manager is aware of the extent and scope of his or her personal responsibility.

However, it should not be thought that budgeting is a panacea for all a firm's problems. The following are some of the limitations of budgets:

1 Budgets are not a substitute for management action – they are plans which require effective action in order to be fulfilled.

2 Planning is not a precise science, and management needs to react to the dynamic environment.

3 Budgeting is a management tool and must not stifle or preclude management initiative.

BUDGET PREPARATION

A budget is prepared for a period, usually a year, broken down into control periods, usually four weeks or a calendar month. Some firms have 'rolling' budgets, in that each quarter a further quarter is added to the annual budget, so that the firm always has one year's budget prepared. The alternative is to prepare budgets for annual periods, and to repeat the process during the term of the current budget. A major advantage of the 'rolling' process is that budget preparation and evaluation become a continuous part of the management process, rather than an annual event, and that changes in both the environment, and in the firm, are constantly monitored and incorporated into budgets.

It must be emphasised that budgeting is a very practical exercise and that it is most unlikely that the immediate future will differ very much from the immediate past. It follows, therefore, that the next budget will be very similar to the most recent results. In other words, tomorrow is a mirror image of today. The benefits of detailed historical records for the basis of planning cannot be over-emphasised.

A further very important point to be made about planning is that the extent to which budgets are achieved is determined by the degree of success in meeting sales budgets and by very tight control of costs.

Budget preparation is not an accounting exercise; the budget officer administers the timetable, which usually starts bottom-up. Individual managers prepare their own plans, in response to objectives and forecasts, and these are then incorporated into functional budgets. Coordination is required, in terms of capacities and resources, and the identification of limiting factors is an important aspect of the budgetary process. If the firm's objectives are to be achieved, then these limiting factors must be eliminated and coordination effected; however, one principal limiting factor will predominate, and the final budget will be constrained by this factor.

A limiting factor will be some aspect of the resources of the firm that is in short supply and which will constrain the firm's plans. It may be that the firm's productive capacity is inadequate to satisfy the market demand, and therefore the sales budget will need to be constrained to take account of the available capacity. It may be that the longer-range objectives will accommodate an increase in this capacity, but in the short term it will predominate over the market demand. One such factor will dominate all others, and this is known as the 'principal budget factor'. In smaller firms (and in not-so-small firms) it is usually the firm's financial resources and thus the cash budget which will be the principal limiting (or budget) factor.

Once all the plans are completed, then these will be aggregated to form a plan of the next year's financial results and these will indicate whether or not the firm's immediate goals are to be achieved. If this is not the case then the budget must be re-evaluated in order to ensure that there are no elements of inefficiency or under-utilisation in the organisation. When this stage has been completed, if the goals are still not achieved then a reappraisal of those goals and longer-term objectives is necessary. Once the budgets are approved then they become the financial plan for the ensuing period. The planning aspect of budgeting is illustrated in Figure 11.2. It will be noted that the corporate objectives predominate and that the sales budget is the first to be prepared. This is usually the case in practice, regardless of the theoretical aspects of the subject. The detail contained in the budget will depend on the nature of the firm's markets, but it is likely to include at least the following (prepared by months):

1 Output by products, by quantity and value.
2 Sales by customers.
3 Sales by representatives (or other sales outlet).

It will be appreciated that budgets are plans that are considered achievable, and that incentives offered to representatives, by way of targets, will necessarily be set at higher levels. Consideration of the above detail will give an appreciation of the control that will arise on a comparison of actual results with the budget. For example, in any particular month the variance (positive or negative) in product output can be identified with specific customers and with specific representatives. Thus a continuing control can be exercised over the achievement of the short-term objectives. Once the

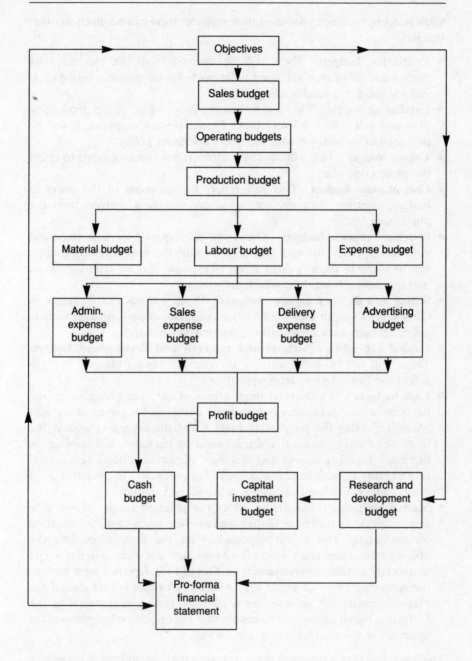

Figure 11.2 Budget schematic

sales budgets have been finalised then consideration can be given to other budgets.

- **Production budgets**   These will be derived from the product sales budget and allowance will need to be made for the manufacturing cycle and for the firm's stockholding policy.
- **Purchasing budget**   This will follow the preparation of the production plan and will reflect delivery times from different suppliers. It will be prepared in accordance with the firm's inventory policy.
- **Labour budget**   This will cover the direct labour requirements to effect the production plan.
- **Cost of sales budget**   This will reflect the outcome of the previous budget, together with the cost of direct materials derived from the purchasing budget.
- **Overhead expense budgets**   These will be prepared for both fixed and variable expenses, for each cost centre within the firm. The opportunity will be taken to identify those items of expense that are controllable by unit managers, from those which are not.
- **Selling and delivery expense budgets**   These will necessarily relate to the levels of output indicated by the sales budget and will also include policy budgets such as advertising and market research.
- **Capital expenditure budgets and research and development budgets**   These will not be influenced by the current annual budget, but will reflect the firm's longer-term objectives.
- **Cash budgets**   The financial implications of all other budgets, i.e. the dates by which customers pay and the demands for payment by suppliers, reflecting the purchasing budget and the inventory policy, the levels of labour utilisation, and remuneration packages, will impinge on the firm's liquid resources and this most important budget reflects the firm's ability to fund its planned level of operations. The preparation of these budgets has been discussed, in detail, in Chapter 6.
- **Master budgets**   These are in effect the planned results of the subsequent period's trading activities, and provide much of the justification for budgeting. This is the opportunity for the firm to consider the efficacy of its operations before the event, and not after, when it would be too late to take corrective action. Figure 11.2 depicts a loop back to the corporate objectives and the implication of this is that should the planned results not achieve the objectives, then a reappraisal of the budgets is required in order to ensure that the operation has planned for optimum levels of efficiency and economy.

The foregoing may have given the impression that the process of budgeting is one of planning output on a scale necessary to achieve certain (subsidiary) objectives e.g. market share, and then of preparing detailed budgets of the operating implications of producing and marketing that output.

However, such a process would negate the aspect of coordination. Implicit in the process of preparing subsequent budgets is that resources exist that can physically and financially support the planned scale of operations.

A predominant feature of the budget process is that of the identification, and elimination, of limiting factors. In the event that resources are not available, then curtailment of the budget is the solution. In any event one such limiting factor will eventually predominate and the final plans will reflect the principal limiting factor.

The above outline is a a very general one and the detailed budgets prepared by firms will reflect both the nature of the individual business and the manner in which it is organised.

ILLUSTRATION

The following example illustrates the broad principles of the detail of budget preparation. It must be remembered that the detail of budget preparation in practice will reflect the individual characteristics of each firm, and greater emphasis will be placed on some budgets than on others.

Three products are produced which are distributed and sold to DIY retailers. Each product utilises a bought-in component, and the manufacturing and assembly is common to all three products.

Table 11.1 provides the budget data for the year to 31 December 19X1. Table 11.2 is the opening balance sheet at 1 January 19X1. Customers, on average, settle 60 per cent of invoices in the quarter in which goods are sold and the remaining 40 per cent in the following quarter.

Component suppliers are paid 60 per cent in the quarter in which the goods are received and 40 per cent in the following quarter.

Variable overheads are paid as the products are produced. Fixed manufacturing overhead is paid in two equal instalments, in quarter 2 and quarter 4. Fixed administration, selling and distribution costs are paid in equal quarterly instalments. From the foregoing information, budgets can be prepared for the ensuing year. These will comprise all the functional budgets, a cash budget and the master budgets, being the final accounts. It is the preparation of these that is the main justification for the planning process, in that an assessment can be made before the year commences of the satisfactory nature of that year's operations. It would be naive indeed to suppose that, merely because activities had been planned in some detail, the results would automatically follow. This will only arise as the result of the control process, which is discussed in the next chapter.

The illustration follows normal practice, which is to commence with the preparation of the sales budget followed by the preparation of the production budget. This procedure illustrates the identification and elimin-

Table 11.1 Data for budget preparation

Selling price:

Product A	£60
Product B	£85
Product C	£80

Sales forecasts (quantities):

	Q1	Q2	Q3	Q4
Product A	20,000	18,000	14,000	20,000
Product B	42,000	46,000	32,000	48,000
Product C	30,000	30,000	30,000	30,000

Stocks of finished goods at 31 December 19X0 were:

Product A	2,000
Product B	6,000
Product C	4,000

The bought-in components are used as follows:

Product	A	B	C	Cost each
Component	3	3	4	£10

Direct labour hours per product are:

Product	A	B	C
Cost £3.00 per hour	4	8	6

Available hours per quarter: 588,000

Overheads:
Variable overheads are absorbed on a direct labour hour basis at £2.00 per labour hour.
Fixed overheads budgeted for the year to 31 December 19X1:

Factory fixed costs	£488,000
Administration, selling and distribution	1,140,000
Depreciation	200,000

ation of limiting factors, in that the sales demand will reflect the seasonality of the market and the requirements of the firm's customers. The production budget will reflect the general inflexibility of the manufacturing resource, and from this budget can be assessed the feasibility of meeting the sales demands, as can requirements in terms of stockholding.

Once the production budget has been finalised, then cost of sales budgets and overhead expenses budgets can be prepared. Finally, the most important cash budget and the master budgets can be produced.

At this point, in practice, ratios will be calculated in order to confirm that the firm's goals towards the long-range objectives are being fulfilled.

The next step is the preparation of the purchases, wages, variable and fixed expenses budgets in relation to the production budget. Once this has been completed then the preparation of the cash budget can be finalised.

Table 11.2 Opening balance sheet

Balance sheet as at 31 December 19X0		
	£000	£000
Fixed assets		1,600
Stocks	800	
Debtors	2,800	
Cash	500	
	4,100	
Less creditors	1,300	
		2,800
Total net assets		4,400
Represented by:		
Ordinary share capital		2,000
Reserves		2,400
Capital employed		4,400

Finally, the budgeted profit and loss account (NB the difference between the production budgets and the cost of sales is the increase or decrease in stocks) can be prepared, together with the budgeted balance sheets. (These are the master budgets.)

SALES AND PRODUCTION BUDGETS

Sales budget

The budget (Table 11.3) shows in detail the quantities and sales value of the sales for each of the products for each quarter. Thus for control purposes a comparison can be made with the actual results, to determine the extent to which quantities budgeted were not achieved (or were over-achieved, as the case may be) and of the prices realised for each product. Budgets are not strait-jackets and must not stifle normal commercial initiatives in the market-place.

Production budget

The problem to be solved is the allocation of the fixed production capacity to the budgeted sales in order to establish stock levels sufficient to meet the budgeted demand (Table 11.4). Thus the production capacity is sufficient to maintain the stocks at the same level at the end of the year as at the start of the year, and to meet the budgeted demand.

Table 11.3 Quarterly sales budgets by products

Sales budget £000	Q1		Q2		Q3		Q4		Total
A 60 (20)	1,200	(18)	1,080	(14)	840	(20)	1,200	(72)	4,320
B (42)	3,570	(46)	3,910	(32)	2,720	(48)	4,080	(168)	14,280
C (30)	2,400	(30)	2,400	(30)	2,400	(30)	2,400	(120)	9,600
	7,170		7,390		5,960		7,680		28,200

Note: The demand in terms of quantities is shown in brackets.

Table 11.4 Annual production requirements in hours

		Output (000s)	Hours (000s)
Product A	(4 hours per product)	72	288
Product B	(8 hours per product)	168	1344
Product C	(6 hours per product)	120	720
Total			2352
per quarter			588

Table 11.5 Quarterly sales budgets in production hours

000 hours	Q1	Q2	Q3	Q4
Product A	80	72	56	80
Product B	336	368	256	384
Product C	180	180	180	180
Total hours required	596	620	492	644
Total hours available	588	588	588	588
Shortfall (excess)	8	32	(96)	56

The next step is to ascertain the seasonality of the sales demand (see Table 11.5) and to allocate the surplus production capacity in order to build the necessary stocks to meet that demand. It can be seen that stocks will need to be reduced during the first two quarters and then that the excess capacity in the third quarter can be used to replenish the reductions and provide for the shortfall in the fourth quarter. Thus the stocks will be restored to the opening quantities. This would not necessarily follow in

Table 11.6 Calculation of production value of opening stocks

A	2,000 units	8,000 hours
B	6,000 units	48,000 hours
C	4,000 units	24,000 hours
		80,000 hours

practice, however, and is merely a device to illustrate the principles in this illustration.

Table 11.6 shows the value in terms of hours (or productive capacity) of the opening stocks. Table 11.7 reveals a production plan (in hours) for each product, for each quarter. The sales figures are the quarterly budget, per product, in hours, and the production figures, in hours, are constant each quarter, which reflects the 'rigidity' of the production capacity. Thus the stock of product A can be used to absorb the shortfall in quarter 1, and part of the stock of product B can be used to absorb the shortfall in quarter 2. The production of A and B can be replenished in quarter 3 and can provide for the excess demand in quarter 4, reinstating the stocks at the end of the year to the same levels as those held at the beginning of the year.

Table 11.7 Quarterly production budgets by products (in hours)

£000	Q1			Q2			Q3			Q4			
	St.	P	Sa	St.	P	Sa	St.	P	Sa	St.	P	Sa	St.
A	8	72	(80)	–	72	(72)	–	72	(56)	16	72	(80)	8
B	48	336	(336)	48	336	(368)	16	336	(256)	96	336	(384)	48
C	24	180	(180)	24	180	(180)	24	180	(180)	24	180	(180)	24

St. = stocks, P = Production, Sa = sales.

In practice, it is unlikely that a firm would allow its stocks to fall to zero. Table 11.8 sets out the quarterly production in terms of hours. Once the production budget has been finalised, the various cost of sales budgets and overhead expenses budgets, based on that level of activity, can be prepared. Although the process may appear complex and overly detailed, this is a crucial element in the rigour of the planning process by coordinating the conflicting demands of the customers with the relative rigidity of the firm's resources.

Table 11.8 Quarterly production budgets in hours

		Annual total
Product A @ £4	18,000	72,000
Product B @ £8	42,000	336,000
Product C @ £6	30,000	180,000
		588,000

Labour budget

Once again, the illustration is an over-simplification of the practical reality of budget preparation, in that no allowance has been made for holiday periods and an assumption, for the purposes of the illustration, has been made that the same hours are available in each quarter.

Table 11.9 Quarterly labour cost budget

£000	Q1	Q2	Q3	Q4	Total
588,000 hours @ £3	1,764	1,764	1,764	1,764	7,056

Purchases budget

The quarterly purchases of the components are shown in Table 11.10. The calculations are the multiplication of the production quantities for each product by the cost of the components used in that product.

Table 11.10 Quarterly purchases budget – components

£000	Q1	Q2	Q3	Q4	Total
Product A	540	540	540	540	2,160
Product B	1,260	1,260	1,260	1,260	5,040
Product C	1,200	1,200	1,200	1,200	4,800
	3,000	3,000	3,000	3,000	12,000

Variable manufacturing overheads budget

Table 11.11 Quarterly variable manufacturing overhead budget

£000	Q1	Q2	Q3	Q4	Total
Variable overheads	1,176	1,176	1,176	1,176	4,704

NB £2 per direct labour hour

Fixed overheads budget

Table 11.12 Quarterly fixed overhead budgets

£000	Q1	Q2	Q3	Q4	Total
Factory	122	122	122	122	488
Depreciation	50	50	50	50	200
Admin., selling & dist.	285	285	285	285	1,140
	457	457	457	457	1,828

Cash budget

It is first necessary to amend the budgeted sales, purchases and expenses to take account of the credit given and taken. This is done as shown in Tables 11.13 and 11.14.

Table 11.13 Calculation of quarterly cash receipts

£000	Q1	Q2	Q3	Q4
1 Receipts				
Sales (£000)	7,170	7,390	5,960	7,680
60%	4,302	4,434	3,576	4,608
40%	2,868	2,956	2,384	3,072
Opening debtors	2,800			
60%	4,302	4,434	3,576	4,608
40%		2,868	2,956	2,384
	7,102	7,302	6,532	6,992
Closing debtors				3,072

Table 11.14 Calculation of quarterly cash payments

	Q1	Q2	Q3	Q4
2 Payments				
Component purchases	3,000	3,000	3,000	3,000
60%	1,800	1,800	1,800	1,800
40%	1,200	1,200	1,200	1,200
Opening creditor	1,300			
60%	1,800	1,800	1,800	1,800
40%		1,200	1,200	1,200
	3,100	3,000	3,000	3,000
Closing creditor				1,200

Table 11.15 Quarterly cash budgets

	Q1	Q2	Q3	Q4
Receipts				
Sales	7,102	7,302	6,532	6,992
Payments				
Purchases	3,100	3,000	3,000	3,000
Wages	1,764	1,764	1,764	1,764
Variable o/hs	1,176	1,176	1,176	1,176
Fix. Fac. o/hs		244		244
Fix. A.S & D o/hs	285	285	285	285
	6325	6469	6225	6469
Surplus (deficit)	777	833	307	523
Surplus (deficit) B/F	500	1,277	2,110	2,417
Surplus (deficit) C/F	1,277	2,110	2,417	2,940

It should be remembered that some of the fixed expenses are paid in the second and fourth quarters.

Master budgets

Finally the preparation of the master budgets can take place, commencing with the profit and loss account. It will first be necessary to satisfy the accounting convention of 'matching' the sales for each quarter with those expenses and costs incurred in producing those sales. In effect, it is necessary to calculate the value of the stock movement which can be adjusted against the costs incurred during that quarter. The next step in the process would be to assess the master budgets, by means of ratio analysis, particularly the return on capital employed, in order to ensure that the planned results were in line with the firm's short-term goals towards its longer-term objectives. However, for the purposes of this example it is sufficient to illustrate the process of preparation.

Table 11.16 Calculation of quarterly stock values

	£000s			
	Q1	Q2	Q3	Q4
1 Calculation of cost of sales				
Production costs				
Purchases	3,000	3,000	3,000	3,000
Labour	1,764	1,764	1,764	1,764
Variable overheads	1,176	1,176	1,176	1,176
	5,940	5,940	5,940	5,940
Cost of sales:				
Variable cost:				
Product A £50	1,000	900	700	1,000
Product B £70	2,940	3,220	2,240	3,360
Product C £70	2,100	2,100	2,100	2,100
	6,040	6,220	5,040	6,460
Stock movement	−100	−280	+900	−520
Stock value	700	420	1,320	800

Table 11.17 Quarterly budgeted profit and loss accounts

	£000				
	Q1	Q2	Q3	Q4	Total
Sales	7,170	7,390	5,960	7,680	28,200
Cost of sales	6,040	6,220	5,040	6,460	23,760
Fixed overhead	457	457	457	457	1,828
	6,497	6,677	5,497	6,917	25,588
Profit	673	713	463	763	2,612

Table 11.18 Quarterly budgeted balance sheets

£000	Q1	Q2	Q3	Q4
Fixed assets	1,550	1,500	1,450	1,400
Stocks	700	420	1,320	800
Debtors	2,868	2,956	2,384	3,072
Cash	1,277	2,110	2,417	2,940
(Creditors)	(1,322)	(1,200)	(1,322)	(1,200)
Net current assets	3,523	4,286	4,799	5,612
Total net assets	5,073	5,786	6,249	7,012
Financed by:				
Issued ordinary shares	2,000	2,000	2,000	2,000
Reserves	3,073	3,786	4,249	5,012
Capital employed	5,073	5,786	6,249	7,012

CONCLUSION

Budgeting is a technique that not only involves planning a firm's activities in considerable detail and giving due regard to constraints, thus coordinating all of the firm's resources, but also provides a mechanism by which the actions of individual managers can be appraised. An important benefit of the application of such a technique is the direction of the firm's most valuable resource – management control – to be directed at those very areas that need attention.

An additional, and not insignificant, benefit arising from the use of this technique is that of the behavioural implications for individual management throughout the firm.

The process of budget preparation directs a manager's attention towards the corporate objectives of the firm and therefore requires that departmental objectives are subordinate to corporate objectives, thus leading towards goal congruence. It is a process that claims to remove conflict between departmental objectives, because all are working towards a common goal. Certainly under a system of budgetary control, corporate goals, and therefore departmental goals, are sharply defined, and actual performance analysed against these standards. It is also a process that requires the total participation of all management in establishing plans for future activities, therefore imposing on them an obligation to accept their individual responsibility towards the achievement of such corporate goals.

It must be appreciated that budgeting is not an accounting process but a management process, and one in which the accounting function takes a passive role, merely representing the 'language' of the technique. What is possibly more pertinent is that budgeting is a *process* of management, not a substitute for management.

KEY LEARNING POINTS

- Planning is a dynamic process that derives from a firm's longer-range objectives and which identifies those objectives for each individual budget-holder.
- Planning facilitates the application of the principle of management by exception.
- Planning incorporates a control loop whereby actual results are continuously compared with the plans.
- Budgets represent a rigorous examination of the firm's resources and its standards of operating efficiency.
- Planning incorporates important behavioural implications for managers by means of compelling coordination of effort, communication and cooperation, resulting in goal congruence.
- Planning is not a panacea, nor is it a substitute for management action.

CASE STUDY

Using the illustration in the chapter as an example, prepare profit budgets for Peter French for the year to 31 December 19X3 on a quarterly basis, and prepare a budgeted balance sheet and cash flow report at the year end.

Calculate the ratios for this year (completing the trend commenced in Chapter 7), and critically appraise the master budgets for the year.

Draft a report to Peter French, identifying the strengths and weaknesses revealed by your analysis.

Chapter 12

Control

INTRODUCTION

There are important behavioural considerations arising from the budgetary process, with its involvement of all levels of management:

- benefit is obtained of individuals' knowledge, experience and initiative;
- morale is boosted;
- individuals are aware of their own particular responsibilities;
- inter-departmental cooperation is fostered;
- all managers are made aware of corporate policies and objectives, and of the problems and difficulties in achieving these;
- performance and efficiency targets implied by the budgets are more readily accepted.

The organisational framework is important to the effectiveness of budgetary control, and clearly defined lines of authority and responsibility are necessary. These also enhance the effectiveness of the budgets as communication channels, both upwards and downwards. The existence of agreed budgets implies cooperation between individuals and departments towards the common goals of the organisation and therefore enhances goal congruence.

Effective budgetary control requires the coordination of departmental objectives and their subordination to the corporate objectives. In order for this to be totally effective it is necessary that the budget represents a goal that is achievable.

A budget is a plan for a period of time. Actual events occur and the comparison of these with the budget may reveal differences (variances) which require investigation and analysis. The result of this will be the implementation of corrective action to eliminate the trend giving rise to an adverse variance. Effective budgetary control involves identifying the variances in time to effect remedial action – determining the cause of the variance and taking the appropriate action promptly.

It must be appreciated that no amount of action can eliminate the variance revealed, as this is historical, but what is important is that its cause is ascertained and corrective action implemented. An efficient manager will already be aware of these forces and will have determined the appropriate course of action. In this event the budget report merely serves as a form of confirmation.

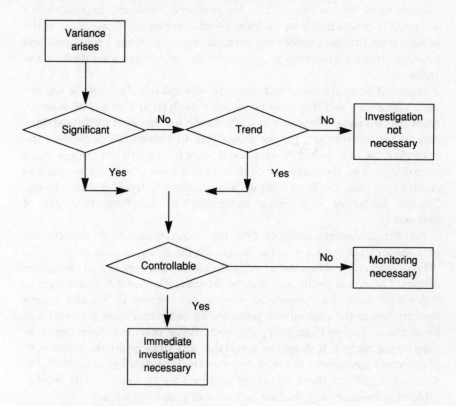

Figure 12.1 Investigating budget variances

Figure 12.1 illustrates a typical set of procedures for variance investigation. If the variance is not significant, or is not part of a trend, then there is no need for further investigation. Thus the principle of materiality, or practicality, is established in that there is no need to spend resources on investigating relatively small differences that are bound to arise. On the other hand, if the variance is significant and is a controllable variance, or if it represents a trend, then either investigation, or monitoring, is required.

FLEXIBLE BUDGETING

The control aspect of budgeting is achieved by comparison of the actual results, for the period, with the budget, and by determining the cause of the difference, or variance. An examination of all the variances will reveal which particular aspect has contributed most significantly to the variation of the actual results from the budgeted plans, and thus the principle of 'management by exception' can be practised, whereby management's attention is concentrated on the most significant factors. Those areas of the organisation that are conforming to the approved plan can be ignored, and policies can be formulated to overcome the difficulties identified by the variances.

It should be appreciated that actual results will not always be in accordance with plans, and that in using variance analysis as a means of management control some allowance must be made for that part of the variance that is 'uncontrollable', having arisen due to circumstances beyond the control of the individual manager responsible for a particular budget. Such variances will be the surpluses or deficits that have arisen due to changes resulting in the levels of output being different from planned levels. Flexible budgeting is a useful technique for identifying this type of variance.

Flexible budgeting involves first the comparison of the budget for planned levels of output with the budget for the actual level of output – the 'flexed' budget – and this will identify the variance arising due to changes in output. The actual results can then be compared with the flexed budget in order to identify the controllable variances, i.e. those differences arising that are under the control and influence of individual managers and that have arisen due to changes in the cost and/or efficiency levels used to prepare the budget. It should be noted that all variances are the responsibility of some manager or function, but that the identification of controllable variances highlights those aspects of performance that are directly attributable to individuals and thus act as a spur to greater efficiency.

The illustration of the advantages of flexible budgeting shows how in the formal presentation of the budget the results of the variance analysis are confused because of the differences between budgeted and actual levels of output. No meaningful control can be exercised through the variances, because like is not being compared with like. In order to identify those variances that are the responsibility of various managers it is necessary to identify those variances that have arisen at the actual level of operations, and not just at the budgeted level. Table 12.1 illustrates the nature of the problem. The accounts show that there has been a shortfall of some £22,000 against the budgeted profit, but do not show how much of this is due to variances arising at the actual level of output and how much arises due to the shortfall in actual output as against budgeted output. (It would

Table 12.1 Monthly budget statement

Department	Month		
	Budget	Actual	Variance
Output (units)	10,000	8,000	2,000
£000			
Sales	100	75	(25)
Variable costs	50	42	8
Contribution	50	33	(17)
Fixed costs	30	35	(5)
Profit (loss)	20	(2)	(22)

Table 12.2 Monthly flexed budget statement

Department	Month		
	Flexed Budget	Actual	Variance
Output (units)	8,000	8,000	
£000			
Sales	80	75	(5)
Variable costs	40	42	(2)
Contribution	40	33	(7)
Fixed costs	30	35	(5)
Profit (loss)	10	(2)	(12)

be equally important to carry out the same analysis if the example had shown a positive variance due to actual output being higher than budgeted output.) The next step is to prepare a flexed budget (Table 12.2) – that is, one that would have been prepared for the actual level of output, and to compare the actual results with the flexed budget to identify the controllable variances. These are the variances that have arisen at the actual level of operations. Clearly, of the original budget some £10,000 of the total variance is due to the shortfall in output, but, more importantly, there has been a £12,000 variance from budget at the actual level of operations. This is a controllable variance and must be analysed and investigated in order to determine the causes.

VARIANCE ANALYSIS

Acceptance of responsibility for performance is an important benefit of budgetary control and it is therefore important that managers are only held responsible for those variances for which they are responsible, and which are controllable.

All variances are controllable, but the allocation of responsibility for these to individual managers is crucial to the success of the system. Flexible budgetary control is a means of achieving this end.

All variances will comprise at least two of the following causes:

- volume;
- price;
- efficiency.

The volume may be higher or lower than the budget, the price may also be higher or lower, and the efficiency may be greater or less than budgeted.

In the previous example the budgets have been prepared from the following data:

- Selling price: £10.00.
- Material cost: 10lb. @ 0.25 pence per lb.
- Labour costs: 30 minutes @ £5.00 per hour.
- Fixed costs: £30,000 per month

In the event, the actual sales were 8,000 units at an average price of £9.375 per unit, 100,000 lb. of material were used at £0.22 pence per lb., and 5,000 hours were recorded at £4.00 per hour. The actual fixed costs were £35,000.

A principle of variance analysis is to always eliminate the price or cost variance first, and then subsequent variances are analysed in budgetary values.

The sales variance will comprise two elements of price and volume. These can be analysed as follows:

- Price: 8,000 units @ (£10.00 – £9.375) = £5,000 (A)
- Volume: 2,000 units @ £10.00 = £20,000 (A)

(The annotation (A) or (F) indicates an adverse or favourable variance.)

The volume variance is the difference between the original budget and the flexed budget, and the causes of this will need to be determined through a detailed examination of the original budget, comparing customer and product budgets with the actual results. This is not in any sense an uncontrollable variance and is the responsibility of the sales function, but its identification and elimination from further effect on other variances, through the mechanism of the flexed budget, does mean that all subsequent variances are controllable, in the sense that they arise from current levels of output. The cause of the price variance will also require explanation as the budgeted price level was £10.00.

An analysis of the expenditure variances can be made, commencing with the materials variance:

- Price: 100,000 lb. @ (25p − 22p) = £3,000 (F)
- Usage: 20,000 lb. @ 25p = £5,000 (A)

The variances reveal that the actual price of the material used was some £3,000 below budget, but that usage was some 20,000 lb. more than budget. The reasons for these variances require explanation, in particular the excess use of materials.

Labour cost variance

- Rate: 5,000 hours @ (£5 − £4) = £5,000 (F)
- Efficiency: 1,000 hours @ £5 = £5,000 (A)

Although the total variance is neutral, both will still require analysis to ascertain why a saving was obtained on budgeted rates and yet there was a significant degree of operating inefficiency.

The fixed costs variance has arisen because of over-expenditure, and the individual cost categories will require examination to determine where this has occurred. Because these costs are fixed, they will arise at budgeted levels regardless of levels of output, and therefore the variance will only be due to over- or under-expenditure, and this will not be influenced by levels of efficiency.

It should be stated that in any reasonably efficient firm, by the time the accounts have been prepared, managers will be aware of the variances and that all the reports will do is to inform them of the precise details. Causes will already have been identified and corrective actions taken.

The monthly budget report will be expanded to include a reconciliation of the budgeted profit with the actual profit in the manner shown in Table 12.3. The report identifies a number of crucial factors. First there is the change in budgeted profit due to the change in the volume of activities, which is the value of the budgeted sales less the variable costs of those sales. This is the profit according to the flexible budget, that is the profit that should have been earned on the actual sales. This is then reconciled with the actual profit per the monthly trading account by summarising the variances calculated for both sales and each cost category.

It is the identification of these factors that allows positive control to be exercised through appropriate strategies to modify their effect. No action can alter the fact of the variances, but action can prevent their arising in the future where they have arisen under controllable circumstances. In an efficient firm these causes will have been identified prior to the preparation of the accounts and actions already devised to counteract their effect. The monthly report will merely confirm the detail.

Table 12.3 Budgeted profit statement

Profit reconciliation		£000	
Budgeted profit			20
Less sales volume variance		20	
Variable cost volume variance		10	10
Profit per flexed budget			10
Less sales price variance		(5)	
Material variances:			
Price	3		
Usage	(5)	(2)	
Labour cost variances:			
Rate	5		
Efficiency	(5)	–	
Fixed cost variances:			
Expenditure		(5)	(12)
Actual loss per accounts			(2)

The layout of the report will reflect both the nature of the firm's activities and its preferences, and will most probably include figures for the year to date.

ILLUSTRATION

A further example can be made by considering the reports that would arise from the illustration given in the previous chapter. In order to compress the detail, only one quarter's results are shown (Table 12.4), but similar reports and analyses would arise from the other quarters. In practice, the management would be receiving reports in respect of various aspects of the firm's activities on a continuous basis, e.g. sales reports monthly and production reports weekly.

Sales for the first quarter were as follows:

Quantity (000s)		*£000*
Product A	22	£1,300
Product B	39	3,200
Product C	34	2,900
		£7,400
Components	319	£3,390
Hours	604	£2,454
Variable overheads		£1,016
Fixed overheads		£520

From the above information, an actual profit statement for the quarter can be prepared, and after analysing the sales variances a flexed budget report can be produced showing the variances that have arisen at the actual levels of production.

Table 12.4 Actual profit and loss account – first quarter

Profit and loss account – first quarter		£000
Sales		7,400
Cost of sales:		
Materials	3,390	
Labour	2,454	
Variable overhead	1,016	6,860
Contribution		540
Less fixed overhead		520
Profit		20

Table 12.5 Sales variance analysis

Variance analysis – sales £000	Total	A	B	C
Budgeted sales	7,170	1,200	3,570	2,400
Actual sales	7,400	1,300	3,200	2,900
Variance	230	100	(370)	500
Price variance				
Actual volumes (000)		22	39	34
@ budgeted prices		1,320	3,315	2,720
actual prices		1,300	3,200	2,900
Total	45	(20)	(115)	180
Volume variance				
Budgeted volumes (000)		20	42	30
Actual volumes		22	39	34
Variance		2	(3)	4
Value (@ budgeted prices)	185	120	(255)	320
Total variance	230	100	(370)	500

In practice, the variance analysis would be much more detailed, giving variances for each of the products. In this example the illustration of this detail has been confined to the sales variance analysis calculation – the cost variances have been shown for the totals only. The budgeted profit for the quarter was £673,000 and the first step in the analysis of the variance is to calculate the sales variances that have arisen due to both volume and price for each of the products. Clearly, although there is an overall favourable variance, investigations will be required to ascertain the reasons for the individual product variances. In the case of product A it would appear that a marginal reduction in the budgeted selling price has been more than offset by an increase in the volumes sold. In the case of product C, both prices achieved and volumes sold are significantly better than budgeted. With product B, however, the reverse is the case, with both prices and volumes significantly below budgeted levels. There could be very many reasons, in practice, why these circumstances have arisen, and careful investigation will be required of the circumstances contributing to the more significant variations. It is the result of these investigations that will determine the actions to be taken in order to rectify the situation in the future. It cannot be stressed too forcibly that no action taken can alter the past results. The efficiency with which such reports are produced will play a very large part in the success of management in controlling the situation in the future.

Cost variances

The first step is to calculate the flexible budgets for each of the cost categories in respect of the actual sales volumes. The flexible budget calculations are merely the recalculation of the original budgeted values (see Chapter 11) against the actual levels of output. These provide the benchmark against which the actual levels of performance can be measured.

The calculation of the individual cost variances can be made in order to determine the causes of any variances. Once again, it is emphasised that these variances are considered controllable because they have arisen, at the actual level of output, against the rigorous standards that prevailed for the preparation of the annual budgets. The material variance analysis (Table 12.7) reveals that there was an overspend of some £200,000, of which some £190,000 was due to price increases, and that some £10,000 arose due to the over-utilisation of components. It has previously been stressed that an efficient management will already be aware of the cause of these variances and will have at least taken steps to prevent, insofar as is possible, their recurrence in the future.

The price variance is calculated by comparing the actual quantity of components used at the budgeted price with the actual cost incurred. The

Table 12.6 Flexible cost budgets

£000	Total	A	B	C
Output for month (000)		22	39	34
Components (£10 each)		3	3	4
Cost per product		£30	£30	£40
Flexible budget	3,190	660	1,170	1,360
Labour hours (£3 per hour)		4	8	6
Cost per product		£12	£24	£18
Flexible budget	1,812	264	936	612
Variable overheads (£2 per labour hour)				
Hours per product		4	8	6
Cost per product		£8	£16	£12
Flexible budget	1,208	176	624	408
Totals	6,210			
Fixed overheads	457			

Table 12.7 Calculation of material variances

Variance analysis (£000)		
Components:		
Flexed budget	3,190	
Actual	3,390	
Variance (adverse)	(200)	
Price:		
Actual quantity @ budget cost (£10)		£3,200
Actual cost		3,390
Price variance (adverse)		(190)
Usage:		
Flexible budget quantities (000)		319
Actual quantities		320
Over-usage		1
Usage variance (1,000 units @ £10 each)		(£10)
Total variance (adverse)		(£200)

Table 12.8 Calculation of labour cost variance

Labour:		
Flexed budget	£1,812	
Actual costs	2,454	
Variance (adverse)	(642)	
Rate:		
Actual hours:		
590 at £3.00 per hour		£1,770
Actual wage payments		£2,454
Rate variance (adverse)		(684)
Efficiency:		
Flexible budget hours		604
Actual hours		590
Under-utilisation		14
Budget variance (favourable)		
@ £3		£42
Total variance (adverse)		(£642)

Table 12.9 Calculation of variable overhead variance

	£000
Flexible budget	£1,208
Actual overheads	1,016
Expenditure variance (favourable)	£192

Table 12.10 Calculation of fixed overhead variance

	£000
Budgeted fixed overheads	457
Actual fixed overheads	520
Fixed overhead variance (adverse)	(63)

usage variance is calculated by comparing the budgeted quantities (the actual output of each product multiplied by the budgeted number of components for each product) with the actual quantities used and multiplying the difference by the budgeted cost per component. The analysis in Table 12.8 shows that there was an adverse variance in respect of wage rates, but that a small favourable variance arose in respect of labour efficiency. Clearly management has to take steps to bring the wage rates under control as there appears to be no correlation between payment above budgeted rates and the increase in productivity. The calculation of the rate variance is made by comparing the actual hours worked valued at the budgeted rates with the actual payments made. The efficiency variance is a comparison of the actual output multiplied by the budgeted number of hours per product with the actual hours taken. In the illustration, the latter are less than the budgeted values and thus show a favourable gain. As the overheads are variable to levels of output, the cause of any variance must be changes to the cost of the various elements of the variable overheads. Therefore the only variance that arises is due to expenditure (Table 12.9). As the fixed overheads do not vary with output, the variance on this budget is also due to expenditure (Table 12.10). The management will need to identify the major elements and to examine the cause of the variances in the actual costs incurred against those budgeted. The calculation is a comparison of the actual output of the products multiplied by the number of hours per product and the rate per hour, with the actual level of expenditure. These rates will have been determined by using the principles outlined in Chapters 8 and 9. Because this element of overhead is fixed, and arises primarily due to the passage of time (see Chapter 8) there can be no variation due simply to changes in levels of output, and consequently the variance will be due to any difference between actual expenditure and the budget. There will be various categories of fixed overhead – salaries, etc., and it will be necessary to extend the analysis to cover all of these in order to determine which categories of fixed cost have contributed to the total variance.

Flexible budget report

The next step is to prepare the flexed budget to provide the information necessary to ascertain the extent to which budgeted figures were achieved in respect of the actual levels of output. Again it must be stressed that these are the variances that would have arisen had the actual levels of output been those that were budgeted. In other words, were the variances to be calculated in respect of the original budget values, then some part of those variances would have arisen in respect of the variation in actual volumes compared with those budgeted.

Table 12.11 Flexed profit statement – first quarter

	£000	
Actual sales		7,400
Less budgeted costs		
Materials	3,190	
Labour	1,812	
Variable overhead	1,208	6,210
Budgeted contribution		1,190
Less budgeted fixed cost		457
Budgeted profit on actual sales		733
Variances:		
Materials		
Price	(190)	
Usage	(10)	(200)
Labour		
Rate	(684)	
Efficiency	42	(642)
Variable overhead		
Expenditure		192
Fixed overhead		
Expenditure		(63)	713
Actual profit for quarter		20

CONCLUSION

Budgeting is a technique that not only involves planning a firm's activities in considerable detail, with due regard to constraints, thus coordinating all of the firm's resources, but also provides a mechanism by which the actions of individual managers can be appraised. An important benefit of the application of such a technique is the direction of the firm's scarcest resource – senior management control – to be directed at those very areas that most need attention.

An additional, and not insignificant, benefit arising from the use of this technique is that of the behavioural implications for individual management throughout the firm.

The process of budget preparation directs a manager's attention towards the corporate objectives of the firm and therefore requires

Table 12.12 Budget figures for 19X2

	£000	
Sales:		
Repairs	120.0	
Contract	50.0	
Manufactured goods	80.0	
Other goods	50.0	
Carpets	30.0	
Curtains	15.0	345.0
Materials Used:		
Repairs	30.0	
Contract	40.0	
Manufactured goods	32.0	
Other goods	33.0	
Carpets	15.0	
Curtains	7.5	157.5
Wages:		
Craftsmen	40.0	
Cleaner	3.2	
Office	8.0	
Retail shop	20.0	71.2
Overheads:		
Subcontract	17.5	
Commissions	5.0	
Rent & rates – unit	5.5	
Rent & rates – storage	1.2	
Rent & rates – shop	4.0	
Heating & lighting – unit	1.0	
Heating & lighting – shop	0.5	
Telephone – unit	1.0	
Telephone – shop	0.5	
Car expenses	2.0	
Van expenses	2.5	
Other expenses	2.0	
Loan interest	6.5	
Lease van	2.4	
Accountancy, etc.	2.5	
Insurances	3.0	
Advertising	6.0	
Depreciation	5.8	
Director's salary	30.0	98.9

that departmental objectives are subordinate to corporate objectives thus leading towards goal congruence.

Budget preparation should have the effect of removing conflict between departmental objectives, because all are working towards a common goal. Certainly under a system of budgetary control, corporate goals, and therefore departmental goals, are sharply defined, and actual performance is analysed against these standards. It is also a process that requires the total participation of all management in establishing plans for future activities and therefore imposes on them an obligation to accept their individual responsibility towards the achievement of such corporate goals.

It must be appreciated that budgeting is not an accounting process but a management process, and one in which the accounting function takes a passive role, merely representing the 'language' of the technique. What is possibly more pertinent is that budgeting is a process of management, not a substitute for management.

Positive planning procedures represent the adoption of a proactive management style of attempting to control the firm's progress towards clear and well-defined objectives. The alternative of operating without such plans is to adopt a reactive style of management and to attempt to control a firm's progress by reacting to each and every shift in the economic and market environment, as and when these occur.

KEY LEARNING POINTS

- **The establishment of budgetary control procedures leads to important behavioural benefits for both the firm and for individual managers.**
- **The technique of flexible budgeting allows for the identification, and control, of those areas of responsibility of individual managers.**
- **This most importantly leads to the congruence of both departmental and corporate goals.**
- **Variance analysis reveals those aspects that have arisen, either positively, or negatively, from an individual manager's performance, and identifies those variances that have arisen due to circumstances beyond their control.**

CASE STUDY

The figures (Table 12.12) were budgeted by Peter French for the year to 31 December 19X2, and the actual results are contained in the case study and have been used for the preparation of his accounts for that year. Prepare a budget report for the year that will enable Peter French to ascertain the extent to which his budgeted profit was achieved and those areas of his business that contributed to this. It will be necessary to consider the manner in which the expenses have been allocated to different profit centres (see Chapter 10), in order to identify any areas that may be of concern.

Chapter 13

Planning and control in divisionalised firms

INTRODUCTION

The problems of control in large firms are often resolved by a process of decentralisation, resulting in the organisation of a number of operating divisions, in which the management has considerably more delegated authority than otherwise exists in smaller concerns. Managements are usually allowed to decide on operating policies, subject only to the constraint of the achievement of overall corporate objectives which are determined at group level. The main impetus of such forms of organisation is the need to make local management aware of their responsibilities in terms of profit and return on investment, and to reduce the size of the operational units to a level at which it is practical to achieve such aims.

The benefits claimed for such organisational structures include the following:

1 Optimal decisions are more likely, as local management is better able to react to local conditions.
2 The burden of decision-making is distributed, leaving group management free to concentrate on strategic decisions.
3 The delegation of authority gives local management greater incentive and motivation.
4 Such delegation provides an effective check on market prices for the transfer of products within the organisation. Divisional managers quickly identify uneconomic activities within the group.
5 Such organisational structures provide better management training in decision-making.

Weaknesses arising from these types of organisational structure have been identified as:

1 dysfunctional decision-making through failure to harmonise divisional activity with corporate goals;
2 duplication of activities across divisions;
3 increased information processing and distribution.

ASSESSMENT OF PERFORMANCE

It is fairly clear that the foregoing refers to a division as part of an organisation that has a considerable degree of control over its own activities. However, the extent to which such autonomy extends in a financial sense will determine whether or not the division is a profit centre or an investment centre. In the first case the division merely controls its own revenues and expenses and is obliged to resort to application to the corporate centre for investment funds. In the latter case the division controls its own investment programme, and by implication, has some autonomy in determining its own level of borrowing.

In the event that an organisation elects for a system of profit centres, then the problems of control are relatively simple. Profit targets are approved at corporate level and performance is monitored by the comparison of actual results against the target or budget. The major concern under these circumstances, at corporate level, will be that profit is essentially a short-run concept and control will need to be exercised in order to ensure that divisional performance is not such as to impair the longer-term corporate objectives. A further matter of concern, referred to in more detail later, arises when a significant amount of inter-divisional trading takes place. The level at which the transfer prices are set can significantly affect the performance of divisions involved in such trading. In the case of profit centres the accounting procedures necessary to determine the divisional profit need to ensure that the level of divisional profit *prior* to the allocation of any general corporate charges is identified, so that the efficiency of divisional performance, in this respect, is known.

The problem of allocation is one that is more pertinent in the case of investment centres, as this involves the twin aspects of cost and investment. The main issue is that of the definition of both the base of investment and the profit from which the level of divisional performance is to be assessed. The inclusion of the allocation of a share of corporate investment and an allocation of a share of corporate overheads would depress the measure of performance by the division and might have the effect of inhibiting divisional management's motivation.

Problems arise in any attempt to assess divisional performance by means of a return ratio, such as return on capital employed (ROCE). Problems associated with the use of a ROCE accounting measure include:

1 Essentially, profit is a short-term measure (the difference between revenues and costs), and its use may cause divisional management to ignore longer-term benefits in favour of the short-term, where these are likely to affect the ratio more favourably.
2 Investment in replacement assets may be delayed in order to favourably affect the the ROCE ratio in the short term.
3 The use of historic cost accounts results in a return that overstates the

real position. Historic costs understate the value of capital employed and overstates the profit, thus overstating the 'real' rate of return.

In an attempt to overcome these problems an approach involving residual income (RI) has been proposed. This involves the assessment of divisional performance in relation to the amount of residual income, which is defined as divisional profit less an imputed interest charge on divisional assets. Obviously the previously mentioned problem of allocation of both costs and investment still arises, but may be overcome by measuring the calculation in relation to purely divisional transactions. (Equally, the ROCE could be dealt with in this way, although the previously mentioned problems would remain.) Table 13.1 illustrates the position in that under the ROCE method of appraisal a division would choose project A, whereas unsing the RI criteria, project B would be preferred. Advocates of RI claim that this method is more akin to the principles of maximising corporate wealth.

Where a firm is organised on a divisional basis, some form of assessment is necessary in order to assess the performances in both relative and absolute terms of the divisional management. It appears that whatever method is selected, some disadvantages will need to be overcome. The major problem of allocation of shared investment and common costs can, to some extent, be overcome by assessment on the basis of divisional investment and divisional transactions. Whether or not this assessment is conducted by means of ROCE or RI seems immaterial, as the important aspect is to operate the division in such a manner that achievement of corporate objectives is maximised.

TRANSFER PRICES

To the extent that inter-divisional trading occurs, the achievement of corporate objectives will not be affected, in that such transactions result in equal levels of revenue and costs in different divisions, but problems may arise if the value of the transactions have a dysfunctional effect on the performance of one division. Should the level of the transfer price between the divisions be such as to materially affect the performance of one of the divisions, then this may have the effect of either distorting the perception of managerial competence at corporate level, or reducing the motivation of the divisional management in the performance of their responsibilities.

There are a number of ways in which the transfer price can be established. The following are the more common.

Market price

In order to be appropriate, the good that is being supplied must be one for which there is a competitive source of supply regularly available. If this is

Table 13.1 Comparison of projects

	Project A £000	Project B £000
Investment	1,000	5,000
Annual return	200	750
Cost of capital 12%		
ROCE	20%	15%
Interest charge	120	600
Residual income	80	150

the case then the supplying division has to provide a service at a competitive price in order to obtain inter-divisional custom. The results of such a division effectively reflect its ability to perform in a competitive environment. The method is, however, difficult to apply where the supply of one division is peculiar to the requirements of another, e.g. the supply of semi-finished components. Under such circumstances a different method of calculation is required.

Marginal cost

Economic theory establishes that this is the correct transfer price, in that it achieves the criteria of goal congruence. It does not, however, assist in performance evaluation in that the supplying division is merely relieved of the marginal cost of supply and does not obtain a contribution towards the cost of capacity provision i.e. fixed costs. The addition of such a contribution may make the supply of the good uneconomic to the recipient division, thus causing the loss of market opportunity, to the detriment of the organisation as a whole. It should be appreciated that the problem that arises is one of possible conflict between divisional autonomy and therefore motivation of divisional management and the corporate objectives of the firm.

A possible solution to the marginal price problem is the adoption of a two-tier method which can be applied where the supply is on a regular basis and also represents a significant proportion of the capacity. Such a method would involve agreement on the proportion of capacity to be utilised and a transfer charge relating to the fixed cost of that capacity. Supply of the goods is then made at marginal cost. The previously mentioned problem of lack of contribution remains and requires resolution.

Cost price plus

This can be defined as cost – either marginal or total – plus an agreed margin for profit. Where such a method is adopted, and the supply represents a significant proportion of the output of the supply division, then the incentive to control costs may be removed from this division. Such a method will have the consequence of transferring the inefficiencies of the supply division to the recipient division. These problems may be overcome by using standard costs rather than actual costs, but this may then lead to dysfunctional decisions. Additionally, the concept of an addition for profit raises the problem of defining what is a reasonable level of profit.

Consider a situation where the market price for a particular product is £800. A component is supplied by division A to division B, who complete and sell the product. Variable costs in division A are £200 and in division B are £400.

At the market price, a contribution to the fixed overheads of both divisions will be made and, dependent on the level of demand, the supply of the product will add to the total level of corporate profit. Whether or not the supply is undertaken will, to a large extent, depend on the price charged by division A to division B. Assuming that divisional autonomy exists (i.e. that decisions are taken by divisional management), a price of more than £400 would render the supply to the market by division B uneconomic – the price would need to be less than £400 in order to make it an economic proposition.

CONCLUSIONS

The problems hitherto discussed arise because of the size of firms which, in order to strengthen their effectiveness, have adopted an organisational structure of divisionalisation or decentralisation, and have delegated to the management of those divisions the authority to take decisions regarding investment and profit, subject only to the need to achieve corporate objectives. It must be recognised that in establishing such an organisational structure, important decisions at divisional level may fail to achieve the desired effect in relation to those objectives.

KEY LEARNING POINTS

- **The problems of large organisations that have decentralised their operations lie in the mechanism selected to evaluate the performance of those subsidiary divisions.**
- **Whatever mechanism is selected, it must be such that corporate, rather than divisional, objectives are satisfied.**
- **Where inter-divisional trading occurs, then the problem of the transfer price assumes a critical importance in the assessment of divisional performance.**

CASE STUDY

Consider the departmental accounts prepared for Peter French for 19X2 and the budgets prepared for 19X3, and prepare a resumé of the appropriate method of evaluating the performance of his various activities. To what extent would it be possible, or desirable, to evaluate these on the basis of return on capital employed? Is it possible to utilise the residual income approach? Would either of these techniques be of any practical use to an entrepreneur like Peter French? If not, why not? What method would give the most effective control?

Whatever the outcome of the previous problem it is a fact that goods are manufactured at his unit and sold in his retail shop. To this extent, if an accounting methodology is adopted for the purpose of control and evaluation it will need to consider the price at which the goods should be transferred from one department to the other. Consider the most appropriate mechanism that should be adopted after giving due consideration to his particular needs and circumstances.

Case study – accounts and transactions

Table A1.1 Audited profit statements, 19X0 and 19X1

Audited accounts

Trading and profit and loss accounts for the year ending 31 December

£000	19X0	19X1
Sales	295.3	314.0
Cost of sales:		
Materials	140.3	142.0
Wages	40.3	42.4
Subcontract	15.8	16.6
Commission	6.0	4.5
Gross profit	92.9	108.5
Less overheads		
Salaries	28.0	29.6
Other	32.0	33.9
Director's salary	20.0	25.0
Operating profit	12.9	20.0
Less interest	7.5	7.0
Profit before taxation	5.4	13.0
Taxation	1.4	3.3
Retained profit	4.0	9.7

Table A1.2 Audited balance sheets, 19X0 and 19X1

Balance Sheet as at 31 December

£000	19X0	19X1
Fixed assets		
Tangible assets	15.9	15.2
Goodwill	50.0	50.0
Total fixed assets	65.9	65.2
Current assets		
Stocks	12.0	13.6
Debtors	3.8	4.0
Cash and bank	−7.8	−1.9
Total current assets	8.0	15.7
Less current liabilities		
Trade creditors and accruals	14.5	14.9
Taxation	1.4	3.3
Total current liabilities	15.9	18.2
Net current assets	−7.9	−2.5
Total assets less current liabilities	58.0	62.7
Less loan	45.0	40.0
Total net assets	13.0	22.7
Financed by:		
Issued ordinary share capital	1.0	1.0
Reserves	12.0	21.7
Shareholders' funds	13.0	22.7
Tangible assets:		
Car (cost)	8.0	8.0
Car (book value)	6.0	4.5
Plant (cost)	16.0	18.0
Plant (book value)	9.9	10.7

Table A1.3 Cash flow reports, 19X0 and 19X1

Cash flow reports year ending 31 December		
£000	*19X0*	*19X1*
Operating profit	12.9	20.0
Add depreciation	3.1	2.7
Less increase (decrease) in working capital	(2.0)	(1.4)
Net cash flow from operating activities	14.0	21.3
Servicing of finance		
Interest paid	7.5	7.0
	6.5	14.3
Taxation paid	1.0	1.4
	5.5	12.9
Investing activities		
Purchase of fixed assets (net)	4.5	2.0
Net cash inflow before financing	1.0	10.9
Financing activities		
Redemption of loan capital	(5.0)	(5.0)
Increase (decrease) in cash resources	(4.0)	5.9

Table A1.4 Detailed transactions, 19X0 and 19X1

Details of the various entries for the two years are:

£000		19X0	19X1
Sales			
Repair		103.4	117.5
Contract		60.0	45.0
Manufactured goods		68.9	76.5
Other goods		35.0	40.0
Carpets		20.0	25.0
Curtains		8.0	10.0
Totals		295.3	314.0
Materials used			
Repair		30.1	33.8
Contract		48.0	36.0
Manufactured goods		24.5	27.6
Other goods		23.7	27.1
Carpets		10.0	12.5
Curtains		4.0	5.0
Totals		140.3	142.0
Salaries			
Office		7.0	7.5
Shop		18.0	18.9
Cleaner		3.0	3.2
Totals		28.0	29.6
Other overheads			
Rent and rates	– unit	5.3	5.4
	– storage	1.2	1.2
	– shop	3.5	4.0
Heating and lighting			
	– unit	0.9	1.0
	– shop	0.7	0.8
Telephone	– unit	0.8	1.0
	– shop	0.3	0.4
Insurance		2.5	2.7
Car expenses		1.5	1.6
Van expenses		1.9	2.3
Van lease		2.4	2.4
Accountancy, etc.		1.5	1.5
Other		1.2	1.3
Depreciation	– car	2.0	1.5
	– plant	1.1	1.2
Advertising		5.2	5.6
Totals		32.0	33.9

Table A1.5 Transactions for 19X2

During the year to 31 December 19X2, the following transactions were recorded:

	£000
Sales	
Repair	122.2
Contract	50.0
Manufactured goods	84.2
Other goods	45.0
Carpets	27.0
Curtains	12.0
Totals	340.4
Materials used	
Repairs	34.8
Contract	40.0
Manufactured goods	28.3
Other goods	30.5
Carpets	13.5
Curtains	6.0
Totals	153.1
Wages	
Craftsmen	44.6
Cleaner	3.2
Office	8.0
Shop	19.8
Totals	75.6
Subcontract	17.5
Commissions	5.0
Overheads	
Rent and rates – unit	5.5
– storage	1.2
– shop	4.0
Heating and lighting – unit	1.1
– shop	0.9
Telephone – unit	1.1
– shop	0.5
Car expenses	1.8
Van expenses	2.5
Other expenses	1.5
Loan interest	6.5
Van lease	2.4
Accountancy, etc.	2.5
Insurances	3.0
Advertising	6.5
Totals	41.0
Director's salary	30.0

Table A1.6 Budgeted transactions for 19X3

During the year a new car was purchased for £15,000 and the old one sold for book value. The old one had been purchased in 19X0 for £8,000. Additional plant was purchased during the year for £2,000. The car is depreciated at 25 per cent per annum by the reducing balance method and plant is depreciated at 10 per cent per annum by the straight-line method.

The following are his budgets for the year to 31 March 19X3:

Sales

Upholstery repair	£131,600
Contracts	50,000
Manufactured goods	91,800
Other goods	45,000
Carpets	30,000
Curtains, etc.	15,000
Total	£363,400

Materials

Repairs	£30,600
Manufactured goods	38,200
Carpets and curtains	22,500
Other goods	30,000

Contracts

Materials, etc.	£40,000
Commissions	5,000

Wages

Craftsmen	£31,200
Assistants	10,400
Retail shop wages	20,000
Cleaner	3,200
Secretary	8,000
Driver and assistant	12,000

Other overheads

Subcontractors		£17,500
Rent and rates	– unit	5,500
Rent and rates	– storage	1,200
Rent and rates	– retail shop	4,000
Lighting and heating	– unit	1,200
Lighting and heating	– shop	1,000
Telephone	– unit	1,200
Telephone	– shop	500
Car expenses		1,800
Van expenses		1,500
Interest		6,000
Miscellaneous expenses		1,700
Depreciation	– car	2,800
Depreciation	– plant	1,600
Lease	– van	2,400
Accountancy and legal fees		2,500
Insurances		3,500
Director's salary		30,000
Advertising		7,200

Capital expenditure

New plant	£3,000

Case study – solutions to exercises

CHAPTER 1 INTRODUCTION

The following books of account will be necessary in order to provide the business with the control functions for cash, payment of wages and salaries, payment of suppliers, and to provide the data for both periodic management reports and for the statutory records for the annual returns and accounts.

1 Cash book(s), suitably analysed to show:
   — receipts from different categories of sales and of any other receipts;
   — payments, analysed between payments to credit suppliers (purchases ledger) and other payments in respect of wages and salaries, Inland Revenue for payroll deductions and contributions, ands for corporation tax, Customs and Excise for VAT liabilities, loan interest and repayment and for other expenditure suitably classified.
2 Petty cash-books, at both the office and the retail shop, for miscellaneous expenditure.
3 Purchases day-book for the monthly recording of purchases on credit.
4 Purchases ledger, with an account for each credit supplier.
5 Payroll for both weekly paid and monthly paid employees, including the director. Weekly and monthly summaries will be required for management control purposes.
6 Nominal ledger where all profit statement and balance sheet accounts are maintained, e.g. sales, share capital, etc.

● **Going concern** The depreciation charge in the profit and loss account and in the balance sheet is an example of how expenditure – in this case, the purchase of fixed assets – can be written off over a number of years into the future.

● **Conservatism** The inclusion of reserves (accruals) which are estimates of expenditure already incurred for which an account has not been received. These are deducted in the profit statement and are shown in the balance sheet under current liabilities.

- **Matching** The deduction of stocks from materials purchased and shown in the balance sheet as an asset under current liabilities. These have been purchased during a financial period, but because they have not been sold, are carried forward into the future until sold, when they will be deducted as a cost and the profit realised shown in the profit statement.
- **Accruals** This convention is illustrated by the inclusion of prepayments under debtors as a current asset. Although rent, rates and insurances have been paid for future periods, because these expire beyond the date of the balance sheet, that portion relating to the period after the date of the accounts is shown as an asset. It is not clear whether the asset represents future services from the landlord or the insurance company, or whether it represents a liability by the future period.
- **Cost** All the values in both reports are evidence of this convention, as they represent the transactions at the cost incurred.

CHAPTER 2 PROFIT STATEMENTS

Table A2.1 Profit statement, 19X2

Trading and profit and loss account for the year ending 31 December 19X2	£000
Sales	340.4
Cost of sales:	
Materials	153.1
Wages	44.6
Subcontract	17.5
Commission	5.0
Gross profit	120.2
Less overheads	
Salaries	31.0
Other	40.3
Director's salary	30.0
Operating profit	18.9
Less interest	6.5
Profit before taxation	12.4
Taxation	3.1
Retained profit	9.3

The other overheads figure is the total of £41,000 (Table A1.5), less the interest of £6,500, plus the depreciation as calculated in Table A2.2.

No advantage would accrue to the director in instituting a policy of dividend distribution, as the profits 'belong' to the ordinary shareholders

Table A2.2 Calculation of depreciation charge

Car: cost	£15,000
Depreciation @ 25% per annum	£3,750
Plant: cost brought forward	£18,000
Additions during year	2,000
	£20,000
Depreciation @ 10% per annum	£2,000
Total depreciation for the year	£5,750

and, as the majority shareholder, he can adjust his salary to accommodate his financial requirements, subject only to the availability of profits. In this example he is very little different from a sole proprietor, whose profits before taxation are treated as his drawings and whose accounts do not show any remuneration.

CHAPTER 3 BALANCE SHEETS

Stocks represent three months' purchases of both manufactured goods and other goods. Debtors are the prepayments in respect of rent and rates (one quarter) and insurances (six months). Creditors represent one-twelfth of all material purchases, one week's wages and one quarter of both heating and lighting and telephone expenses.

The important values in the above balance sheet are:

	£000
Capital employed	67.0
Fixed assets	71.9
Net current assets (working capital)	−4.9
Loan capital	35.0
Shareholders' funds	32.0

In the case of a publicly quoted limited company, such as Marks and Spencers, it is relatively simple to determine the market value of the business, it is the multiplication of the stock market price per share by the number of shares issued. This valuation process cannot be applied to privately owned companies' whose shares are literally worth the value agreed between a willing buyer and a willing seller.

Whereas the balance sheet value of each £1 share is £32.00, the value placed on them by a purchaser is more likely to be related to the operating profit. In effect, the purchase of all the shares would be the purchase of this profit potential. In addition the purchaser would need to adjust this figure by the cost of employing new managers in place of the present owner/manager. The resultant figure would represent the purchaser's return on

Table A2.3 Balance sheet, 19X2

Balance sheet as at 31 December 19X2		£000
Fixed assets		
Tangible assets		21.9
Goodwill		50.0
Total fixed assets		71.9
Current assets		
Stocks	14.7	
Debtors	4.2	
Total current assets	18.9	
Less current liabilities		
Overdraft	3.6	
Trade creditors and accruals	17.1	
Taxation	3.1	23.8
Net current assets		−4.9
Total assets less current liabilities		67.0
Less loan		35.0
Total net assets		32.0
Financed by:		
Issued ordinary share capital		1.0
Profit and loss account		31.0
Shareholders' funds		32.0
Tangible assets:		
Car (cost)		15.0
Car (book value)		11.2
Plant (cost)		20.0
Plant (book value)		10.7

his investment and would therefore be determined by the rate of return required. If a return of 25% was required, then the adjusted profit figure would be multiplied by four to obtain the valuation. A further complication arises, in that the profits being purchased are not the historic ones but those that will arise in the future.

From the vendor's point of view the adjusted profits (operating profits plus the director's salary) represent the return on an investment of both cash and effort over time and will therefore represent the return required from the sale price. If a 'safe' investment yields, say, 10% before tax, then this adjusted figure needs multiplying by ten to obtain the asking price for all the share capital. It is very probable that the two valuation processes will produce widely differing valuations. Such is the nature of negotiations.

CHAPTER 4 CASH FLOW REPORTS

Table A2.4 Cash flow report, 19X2

Cash flow report for the year ended 31 December 19X2	£000
Operating profit	18.9
Add depreciation	5.8
Less increase (decrease) in working capital	(0.9)
Net cash flow from operating activities	25.6
Servicing of finance:	
Interest paid	6.5
	19.1
Taxation paid	3.3
	15.8
Investing activities:	
Purchase of fixed assets	12.5
Net cash flow before financing	3.3
Less loan capital repaid	5.0
Decrease in cash resources	−1.7

The utility of the cash flow report is succinctly identified, in that although the profit statement reports an operating profit of some £18,900, the cash resources have fallen by £1,700, i.e. the overdraft has increased to £3,600.

Thus the statement identifies the essential factors that have arisen, namely the purchase of fixed assets, the redemption of the loan capital, together with the payment of loan interest and taxation which are deducted from the operating profit in the profit statement. Additionally it disregards the accounting conventions and 'adds back' the net decrease in working capital. Thus it essentially justifies the contention 'profit is opinion but cash is fact'.

CHAPTER 5 ACCOUNTING FOR INFLATION

Neither formal financial statements nor internal management accounts adjusted for inflation, by any method, would be of great value to the owner/manager of a small business. Although the claims made for this approach may have some utility for an investor or other reader or analyst of the financial reports of large companies such a report would not assist an owner in the decision-making process. The majority of decisions made by such owners are essentially short-term and would not be affected, to any material extent, by inflation. In any event the decisions, even where of a longer-term nature, would be made for strategic reasons, and would of themselves take likely trends in inflation into account. The shorter-term decisions would also be made against the background knowledge of such trends.

CHAPTER 6 CASH FORECASTING

Table A2.5 Cash budget, 19X3

Quarterly cash budget year to 31 December 19X3

£000	Q1	Q2	Q3	Q4	Total
Receipts					
Sales	90,850	90,850	90,850	90,850	363,400
Payments					
Suppliers[1]	42,225	40,325	40,325	40,325	163,200
Commissions	1,250	1,250	1,250	1,250	5,000
Wages[2]	13,300	13,400	13,400	13,400	53,500
Salaries	7,800	7,800	7,800	7,800	31,200
Subcontract	4,375	4,375	4,375	4,375	17,500
Rates	1,250		1,250		2,500
Rent	2,050	2,050	2,050	2,350	8,500
Light and heating[3]	500	550	550	550	2,150
Telephone[3]	400	425	425	425	1,675
Advertising	1,800	1,800	1,800	1,800	7,200
Insurances			3,500		3,500
Accountancy		2,500			2,500
Car expenses	450	450	450	450	1,800
Van expenses	375	375	375	375	1,500
Lease van	600	600	600	600	2,400
Miscellaneous expenses	425	425	425	425	1,700
Director's salary	7,500	7,500	7,500	7,500	30,000
Taxation		3,100			3,100
Plant		3,000			3,000
Loan repayments	1,250	1,250	1,250	1,250	5,000
Loan interest	1,500	1,500	1,500	1,500	6,000
Total payments	87,050	92,675	88,825	84,375	352,925
Surplus (deficit)	3,800	(1,825)	2,025	6,475	10,475
Balance b/forward	(3,600)	200	(1,625)	400	(3,600)
Balance c/forward	200	(1,625)	400	6,875	6,875

The detail contained in the cash budget, together with the necessary adjustments, reflects both the importance and complexity of this document. It has previously been stated that the complexities that would arise in respect of both value added tax and of deductions of income tax and graduated insurance contributions from wages and salaries has been ignored.

1 The calculation of payments made to suppliers needs to follow the calculation of the purchases, which will reflect the stockholding of three months of manufactured goods and of goods purchased for resale. The principles behind these calculations are illustrated in Chapter 2. It

should be noted that, in practice, the values shown would be different from month to month to reflect both any seasonality of demand and differences in types of products stocked.

Table A2.6 Calculation of quarterly payments to suppliers

Calculation of stocks:	Q1	Q2	Q3	Q4
Cost of goods sold	40,325	40,325	40,325	40,325
Add stock at end	17,200	17,200	17,200	17,200
	57,525	57,525	57,525	57,525
Less stock at start	14,700	17,200	17,200	17,200
Goods purchased	42,825	40,325	40,325	40,325
Add creditors at start	12,800	13,400	13,400	13,400
	55,625	53,725	53,725	53,725
Less creditors at end	13,400	13,400	13,400	13,400
Payments	42,225	40,325	40,325	40,325

2 Wages

Table A2.7 Calculation of wage payments

	Q1	Q2	Q3	Q4
Wages earned	13,400	13,400	13,400	13,400
Add creditor at start	900	1,000	1,000	1,000
	14,300	14,400	14,400	14,400
Less creditor at end	1,000	1,000	1,000	1,000
Payments	13,300	13,400	13,400	13,400

3 In the case of both lighting and heating, and telephone the payment in the first quarter will be of the accrual at December 19X2.

CHAPTER 7 INTERPRETATION OF FINANCIAL REPORTS

Commentary

The ROCE has improved significantly over the three years, but has fallen slightly in 19X2 mainly due to a fall in the margin on sales, which had also improved in 19X1. There has been no change in the efficiency of the utilisation of capital employed.

Table A2.8 Ratio analyses 19X0, 19X1 and 19X2

Ratio analysis, year ending 31 December	19X0	19X1	19X2
Prime ratios			
ROCE (%)	22.2	31.9	28.2
Margin on sales (%)	4.4	6.4	5.6
Capital turnover	5.1	5.0	5.1
Gearing (% of capital employed)	77.6	63.8	52.2
Return on shareholders' funds (%)	41.5	57.3	38.8
Stability			
Solvency	0.67	0.87	0.79
Liquidity	0.16	0.20	0.18
Profitability (all percentages)			
Cost of sales			
Materials	47.5	45.2	45.0
Wages	13.6	13.5	13.1
Subcontract	5.4	5.3	5.1
Commission	2.0	1.4	1.5
Gross profit	31.5	34.5	35.3
Salaries	9.5	9.4	9.1
Other overheads	10.8	10.8	11.8
Director's salary	6.8	8.0	8.8
Other overheads			
Rent and rates	3.4	3.4	3.1
Heating and lighting	0.5	0.6	0.6
Telephone	0.4	0.4	0.5
Car expenses	0.5	0.5	0.5
Van expenses	0.6	0.7	0.7
Lease – van	0.8	0.8	0.7
Advertising	1.8	1.8	1.9
Miscellaneous expenses	0.4	0.4	0.4
Accountancy, etc.	0.5	0.5	0.5
Insurances	0.8	0.9	0.9
Depreciation	1.0	0.9	1.7
Sales mix			
Repair	35.0	37.4	35.9
Contract	20.3	14.3	14.7
Manufactured goods	23.3	24.4	24.7
Other goods	11.9	12.7	13.2
Carpets	6.8	8.0	7.9
Curtains	2.7	3.2	3.5
Productivity			
Sales per employee	26.85	28.55	30.95
Sales per £ remuneration[1]	3.34	3.24	3.22
Sales per £ remuneration[2]	2.84	2.76	2.77
Performance			
Sales/fixed assets (exc. goodwill)	18.6	20.7	15.5
Sales/stocks	24.6	23.1	23.2
Sales/trade creditors	20.4	21.1	21.0
Working capital ratios –			
Time (days) (312 days per annum)			
Stocks	12.7	13.5	13.4
Creditors	15.3	14.8	14.9

Notes: [1] Excluding subcontract;   [2] Including subcontract

The regular reduction in the bank loan is reducing the degree of gearing, which is consequently causing reductions in the return on shareholders' funds. This will eventually converge with the ROCE when the loan is repaid.

Both the solvency and liquidity positions are very grave, and the company clearly needs an injection of equity capital in order to redress this position. Either a reduction in stockholding, which may affect the level of sales in the retail outlet, or an extension of the credit taken from suppliers, which is, in itself, an unwise policy, are required in order to alleviate the liquidity position.

An examination of the profitability ratios reveals that the main cause of the improvement in net profit margins is a continuing improvement in the gross profit margins, because of the reduction in the material percentage of sales. This, as shown by the sales mix analysis, is due to the increase in sales of both manufactured goods and of purchased goods for resale. Overhead costs are increasing and the cause of this is the director's salary and the increase in the depreciation charge, which in itself is due to the purchase of the director's car.

One cause for concern is revealed by the productivity ratios which, although showing an improving trend of sales per employee, do show that costs of employment (both including and excluding subcontract costs) reveal a downward trend. The director is an integral part of the team and it is interesting that this cost is the significant cause of the deterioration.

The efficiency of the employment of capital is constant and an analysis reveals that the investment in fixed assets has reduced, mainly due to the purchase of the director's car. Both the investment in stocks and the use of creditor finance remain reasonably constant.

(It should be noted that as debtors are merely prepayments, no attempt has been made to either calculate the ratios or to comment on them.)

CHAPTER 8 PRODUCT COSTS

The overhead allocation sheet is prepared in respect of indirect overheads. This is shown in Table A2.9. The following bases have been used for the allocation of indirect overheads:
- Rent and rates, and heating and lighting: area occupied.
- Director's salary and car expenses: equally between administration and selling and delivery.
- Insurances have been shared equally between the two operations.

Recovery rates

Some 7,000 labour hours are booked to jobs during the year and this gives rise to a labour hour recovery rate for the production department of, say,

Table A2.9 Indirect overhead allocation

Indirect overhead allocation for the year ended 31 December 19X3

£000	Total	Unit			Shop	Selling and delivery
		Works	Canteen	Office		
Indirect						
Wages (1/3 × £41,600)	13.9	13.9				
Shop wages	20.0				20.0	
Cleaner	3.2		3.2			
Secretary	8.0			8.0		
Driver and assistant	12.0					12.0
Rent and rates:						
Unit	5.5	4.1	0.6	0.8		
Storage	1.2					1.2
Shop	4.0				4.0	
Heat and Light:						
Unit	1.2	0.9	0.1	0.2		
Shop	1.0				1.0	
Telephone:						
Unit	1.2			1.2		
Shop	0.5				0.5	
Car expenses	1.8			0.9		0.9
Van expenses	1.5					1.5
Miscellaneous expenses	1.7			1.7		
Depreciation – car	2.8			1.4		1.4
Depreciation – plant	1.6	1.6				
Lease van	2.4					2.4
Accountancy, etc.	2.5			2.5		
Insurances	3.5			3.5		
Director's salary	30.0			15.0		15.0
Advertising	7.2					7.2
Totals	126.7	20.5	3.9	33.2	27.5	41.6
Reallocation of canteen		2.1	(3.9)	0.9		0.9
Totals	126.7	22.6		34.1	27.5	42.5

£3.25 per labour hour. (This is calculated by dividing the department's overheads of £22,600 by 7,000.)

Plusages for both administration and for selling and delivery expenses can be calculated as shown in Tables A2.10 and A2.11.

CHAPTER 9 COST BEHAVIOUR

The extent to which any part of those costs which have been treated as fixed is variable can be determined by the use of regression analysis. To do this would require detailed monthly figures for a period of at least twelve months.

Table A2.10 Calculation of recovery rates

	£
Direct costs	
Materials – Repair	30,600
– Manufactured goods	38,200
	68,800
Wages (£41,600–13,900)	27,700
Prime cost	96,500
Works indirect overheads	22,600
Works cost	119,100
Administration overheads	34,100
Cost of production	153,200
Selling and distribution overheads	42,500
Total costs	195,700
Administration plusage to works cost, say	29%
Selling and distribution plusage to cost of production, say	28%

Table A2.11 Calculation of job costs

Job costs	Balmoral £	Sandringham £
Direct materials	250.00	300.00
Direct wages	80.00	100.00
Prime cost	330.00	400.00
Works overhead	65.00	81.25
Works cost	395.00	481.25
Administration overhead	114.55	139.56
Cost of production	509.55	620.81
Selling and distribution overhead	152.87	173.83
Total cost	662.42	794.64
Profit 10%	66.24	79.46
Selling price	728.66	874.10
say	750.00	900.00

Table A2.12 Break-even points

£000	19X0	%	19X1	%	19X2	%
Sales	295.3		314.0		340.4	
Variable costs:						
Materials	140.3		142.0		153.1	
Subcontract	15.8		16.6		17.5	
Commission	6.0		4.5		5.0	
Total variable costs	162.1		163.1		175.6	
Contribution	133.2	45.1	150.9	48.1	164.8	48.4
Fixed costs	115.1		125.3		145.9	
Profit	18.1		25.6		18.9	
Break-even point (sales)	255.2		260.5		288.0	
Margin of safety	13.6%		17.0%		15.4%	

Because of the nature of the business, an assumption has been made that only materials, subcontract labour and commissions are variable.

The analysis reveals that contribution margins are improving over the period and that the margin of safety is very realistic for a small business of this size.

CHAPTER 10   COSTS FOR DECISIONS

Table A2.13 Departmental profit statement, 19X2

Departmental profit statement, year to 31 December 19X2				
£000	Total	Prodtn.	Cont.	Purchases
Sales	340.4	206.4	50.0	84.0
Variable costs:				
Materials	153.1	63.1	40.0	50.0
Commission	5.0		5.0	
Subcontract	17.5	17.5		
Total variable costs	175.6	80.6	45.0	50.0
Contribution	164.8	125.8	5.0	34.0
Less fixed costs	145.9			
Profit	18.9			
Contribution %	57.7	60.9	10.0	40.5

Table A2.14 Product mix analyses, 19X0, 19X1 and 19X2

£000	Sales	%	Contribution	%
Product mix analysis, 19X0				
Manufacturing	172.3	58.3	101.9	76.5
Contract	60.0	20.3	6.0	4.5
Resale	63.0	21.4	25.3	19.0
Totals	295.3		133.2	
Product mix analysis, 19X1				
Manufacturing	194.0	61.8	116.0	76.9
Contract	45.0	14.3	4.5	3.0
Resale	75.0	23.9	30.4	20.1
Totals	314.0		150.9	
Product mix analysis 19X2				
Manufacturing	206.4	60.6	125.8	76.3
Contract	50.0	14.7	5.0	3.0
Resale	84.0	24.7	34.0	20.7
Totals	340.4		164.8	

It should be noted that wages have been treated as a fixed cost because there is insufficient detail to ascertain the degree of variability of this cost item. Nor is it possible to determine the contribution earned on repair or manufactured goods for resale without details of wage and subcontract costs for these particular items. Further that no attempt has been made to show the fixed cost arising at the retail outlet because, again, insufficient detail is available regarding the usage of the selling and distribution costs attributable to this operation. Generally fixed costs for this and for administration arise in respect of the operation as a whole and the most significant measure of departmental profitability is contribution.

In this regard it can be seen that both aspects, manufacturing and retail, produce satisfactory margins of contribution, and that contract refurbishments which are an ancillary operation which do not involve the investment of capital produce a small contribution to operating profits. The analysis reveals that repair and manufacture produces the most significant amount of total contribution, followed by the retail operation, and that the relative proportions have been maintained over the period.

The rates of contribution earned are shown in Table A2.15. Contribution earned on the main operation has improved marginally over the period, but it should be recalled that this is very dependent on productivity, and that wages have been treated as a fixed cost. Profitability at the retail operation is remarkably consistent.

Table A2.15 Product profitability

%	19X0	19X1	19X2
Production	59.1	59.8	60.9
Contract	10.0	10.0	10.0
Resale	40.2	40.5	40.5

The correct approach to the determination of a selling price for long-standing and redundant stock is at any price above variable costs, which in this case would be the purchase price. Where such items are to be delivered to the customer, then an allowance for this cost must be added to the variable cost, as should any commission payable to retail staff on the sale. The most important feature of these decisions is not the profit margin earned, but the release of valuable working capital which can then be utilised for the purchase of other goods for resale.

This type of sale is a constantly recurring factor in these types of operations and arises mainly because of the difficulty of forecasting demand accurately.

CHAPTER 11 PLANNING

NB A cash budget for the year was prepared as the exercise in Chapter 6.

There is an improvement in the ROCE mainly due to an improvement in profit margins. Capital turnover shows a slight reduction, the cause of which can be determined from the interpretation of the performance ratios. Gearing continues to fall with the programme of loan repayment.

The most significant improvement is in the area of solvency and liquidity, and clearly if present trends continue then the business will begin to generate a substantial cash surplus over the next few years. In order to ascertain the extent of this, forecasts of probable sales levels and associated profit levels should be undertaken.

There is a small fall in the gross profit percentage, due to an increase in the wages percentage. The improvement in profit margins is due to the reduction of overhead costs which arises mainly because these are relatively fixed, and because turnover has increased. One expense to monitor closely is advertising, which is an exception to this comment. The sales mix remains relatively constant, with the decline in contract refurbishment continuing.

One cause for concern is the productivity of the investment in wage remuneration, which continues on a downward trend, albeit a gentle one. Nonetheless, in the light of the previous comment and this ratio, this is an area that should be monitored both carefully and constantly.

Table A2.16 Budgeted profit statement, 19X3

Budgeted profit statements, year ending 31 December 19X3		
£000	*per quarter*	*Total*
Sales	90.9	363.4
Cost of sales		
Materials	40.3	161.3
Commission	1.3	5.0
Subcontract	4.4	17.5
Wages	13.4	53.6
Gross profit	31.5	126.0
Less overheads		
Salaries	7.8	31.2
Other	9.9	39.6
Director's salary	7.5	30.0
Operating profit	6.3	25.2
Less interest	1.5	6.0
Profit before taxation	4.8	19.2
Taxation		4.8
Retained profit		14.4
Other overheads:		
Rent and rates	2.7	10.7
Lighting and heating	0.5	2.2
Telephone	0.4	1.7
Car expenses	0.5	1.8
Van expenses	0.4	1.5
Lease van	0.6	2.4
Other	0.4	1.7
Depreciation	1.1	4.4
Accountancy	0.6	2.5
Insurances	0.9	3.5
Advertising	1.8	7.2
Totals	9.9	39.6

The efficiency of the use of fixed assets improves and is not a matter of major importance in this type of business, but the area of stock investment again shows a marginal decline. This is another area that should be monitored carefully.

It must be stressed that the above analysis, and commentary, for 19X3 is of the budgets for this year. The achievement of the actual figures for the year is a matter of management expertise and the advantage of the technique of budgetary planning is evidenced by the fact that areas of concern have been highlighted and can be monitored during the year in order to improve on the planned outcomes.

Table A2.17 Budgeted balance sheet, 19X3

Budgeted balance sheet as at 31 December 19X3			£000
Fixed assets			
Tangible assets			20.5
Goodwill			50.0
			70.5
Current assets			
Stock		17.2	
Debtors		4.5	
Cash		6.9	
		28.6	
Less current liabilities			
Creditors and accruals	17.9		
Taxation	4.8	22.7	
Net current assets			5.9
Total assets less current liabilities			76.4
Less loan			30.0
Total net assets			46.4
Financed by:			
Issued ordinary share capital			1.0
Profit and loss account			45.4
Shareholders' funds			46.4

Table A2.18 Budgeted cash flow report, 19X3

Cash flow report for the year ending 31 December 19X3	£000
Operating profit	25.2
Add depreciation	4.4
Less increase (decrease) in working capital	2.0
Net cash flow from operating activities	27.6
Servicing of finance	
Interest paid	6.0
	21.6
Taxation paid	3.1
	18.5
Investing activities	
Purchase of fixed assets	3.0
Net cash inflow before financing	15.5
Redemption of loan capital	5.0
Increase in cash resources	10.5

Table A2.19 Ratio analysis 19X3

Ratio analysis, year ending 31 December	19X0	19X1	19X2	19X3
Prime ratios				
ROCE (%)	22.2	31.9	28.2	32.3
Margin on sales (%)	4.4	6.4	5.6	6.9
Capital turnover	5.1	5.0	5.1	4.8
Gearing (% to capital employed)	77.6	63.8	52.2	39.3
Return on shareholders' funds (%)	41.5	57.3	38.8	41.4
Stability				
Solvency	0.67	0.87	0.79	1.3
Liquidity	0.16	0.20	0.18	0.9
Profitability (all %)				
Cost of sales:				
Materials	47.5	45.2	45.0	44.4
Wages	13.6	13.5	13.1	14.7
Subcontract	5.4	5.3	5.1	4.8
Commission	2.0	1.4	1.5	1.4
Gross profit	31.5	34.5	35.3	34.7
Salaries	9.5	9.4	9.1	8.6
Other overheads	10.8	10.8	11.8	10.9
Director's salary	6.8	8.0	8.8	8.3
Other overheads				
Rent and rates	3.4	3.4	3.1	2.9
Heating and lighting	0.5	0.6	0.6	0.6
Telephone	0.4	0.4	0.5	0.4
Car expenses	0.5	0.5	0.5	0.5
Van expenses	0.6	0.7	0.7	0.4
Lease – van	0.8	0.8	0.7	0.7
Advertising	1.8	1.8	1.9	2.0
Miscellaneous expenses	0.4	0.4	0.4	0.5
Accountancy, etc.	0.5	0.5	0.5	0.7
Insurances	0.8	0.9	0.9	1.0
Depreciation	1.0	0.9	1.7	1.2
Sales mix				
Repair	35.0	37.4	35.9	36.2
Contract	20.3	14.3	14.7	13.7
Manufactured goods	23.3	24.4	24.7	25.3
Other goods	11.9	12.7	13.2	12.4
Carpets	6.8	8.0	7.9	8.3
Curtains	2.7	3.2	3.5	4.1
Productivity				
Sales per employee	26.85	28.55	30.95	33.04
Sales per £ remuneration[1]	3.34	3.24	3.22	3.16
Sales per £ remuneration[2]	2.84	2.76	2.77	2.75
Performance				
Sales/fixed assets				
(exc. goodwill)	18.6	20.7	15.5	17.7
Sales/stocks	24.6	23.1	23.2	21.1
Sales/trade creditors	20.4	21.1	21.0	20.3
Working capital ratios – time (days)				
(312 days per annum)				
Stocks	12.7	13.5	13.4	14.8
Creditors	15.3	14.8	14.9	15.4

Notes: [1]Excluding subcontract;   [2]Including subcontract

CHAPTER 12 CONTROL

Clearly, the most significant factor in the shortfall of budgeted profit of £5,000 was the adverse variance on sales. This was offset by an improvement in the actual cost of materials, and wages costs were significantly above budget. This latter aspect is a matter of ongoing concern. There were no significant variances arising on overheads. This would be monitored, in practice, to ensure that an adverse variance was not being masked by a positive one. There are no variances of any particular significance.

Budget reports can be prepared in respect of the previously prepared departmental analysis in Chapter 10. The variances identified in the profit statement are clarified and it can be seen that the shortfall in sales arises due to a very large shortfall in sales of purchased goods, whereas the actual sales for repair and manufacture were marginally in excess of budget. This adverse variance was offset to a large extent by the savings on goods purchased, and the shortfall in budgeted operating profit can be identified with the adverse variance arising on wages.

CHAPTER 13 DIVISIONALISED COMPANIES

None of the activities in the business can be classified as divisions in the sense of there being a need to appraise the performance of the management of that activity. Essentially all of the enterprise is under the proprietor's control. Under these circumstances neither the ROCE nor RI methods would be appropriate. The utilisation of ROCE for the business as a whole is the most appropriate method of performance appraisal.

However, the manufacture of goods for resale at the manufacturing unit does give rise to problems of control and it would be desirable to adopt a transfer price mechanism in respect of these goods. Perhaps the most appropriate would be the prime cost plus an addition for the fixed element of works overheads. A choice of policies could then be considered. First a transfer at this price, which would leave all the profit on the resale at the retail outlet, but yet remove those fixed overheads relating to this production from the manufacturing unit. The departmental profit at this unit would then arise solely from the repair activity. Alternatively, the profit could be shared between the repair and resale activities, although this might result in the appraisal of the two activities, giving conflicting results depending on the level of manufacture for resale.

Table A2.20 Budget report, 19X2

Profit statement: Year to 31 December, 19X2

£000	Budget	Actual	Variance
Sales	345.0	340.4	(4.6)
Cost of sales			
Materials	157.5	153.1	4.4
Wages	40.0	44.6	(4.6)
Subcontract	17.5	17.5	
Commission	5.0	5.0	
Gross profit	125.0	120.2	(4.8)
Less overheads			
Salaries	31.2	31.0	0.2
Other	39.9	40.3	(0.4)
Director's salary	30.0	30.0	
Operating profit	23.9	18.9	(5.0)
Less interest	6.5	6.5	
Profit before taxation	17.4	12.4	(5.0)

Table A2.21 Overhead variances, 19X2

£000	Budget	Actual	Variance
Rent and rates	10.7	10.7	
Lighting and heating	1.5	2.0	(0.5)
Telephone	1.5	1.6	(0.1)
Car expenses	2.0	1.8	0.2
Van expenses	2.5	2.5	
Lease van	2.4	2.4	
Advertising	6.0	6.5	(0.5)
Depreciation	5.8	5.8	
Miscellaneous	2.0	1.5	0.5
Accountancy, etc.	2.5	2.5	
Insurances	3.0	3.0	
Totals	39.9	40.3	(0.4)

Table A2.22 Departmental budget report 19X2

£000	Budget	Actual	Variance
Production			
Sales	200.0	206.4	6.4
Variable costs			
Materials	62.0	63.1	(1.1)
Subcontract	17.5	17.5	
Total	79.5	80.6	(1.1)
Contribution	120.5	125.8	5.3
Contract			
Sales	50.0	50.0	
Variable costs			
Materials	40.0	40.0	
Commission	5.0	5.0	
Total	45.0	45.0	
Contribution	5.0	5.0	
Resale			
Sales	95.0	84.0	(11.0)
Variable costs			
Materials	55.5	50.0	5.5
Contribution	39.5	34.0	(5.5)
Total contribution	165.0	164.8	(0.2)
Less fixed costs	141.1	145.9	(4.8)
Operating profit	23.9	18.9	(5.0)

Glossary

Accounting Standards Board (ASB)
The accounting authority responsible for the issue of Financial Reporting Standards (FRS) and Statements of Standard Accounting Practice (SSAP).

Administrative costs (Administration costs), Administration overheads (Administration oncost)
Those costs incurred by a business in connection with administrative functions.

After tax profits
An alternative term to 'profits after taxation', which are the 'earnings' of a company.

Assets
Long-term (more than one year) purchases by a business of items necessary for the conduct of the business. These include property, manufacturing plant and equipment, office furniture and fixtures and motor vehicles. Assets also include stocks of goods for resale, partly completed manufactured goods and stocks of raw material, moneys owing by customers in respect of credit sales (*debtors*) and cash.

Auditors
Professional accountants appointed by the members (shareholders) of a limited company to audit (check) the annual accounts of that company. All limited companies must have their annual accounts certified by an auditor.

Authorised share capital
The total amount of share capital that a limited company may issue. The amount can be increased if approved by a majority of the shareholders.

Bad debts
Amounts owing by customers, in respect of credit sales, that are irrecoverable.

Borrowed capital
The loan capital of a business.

Called-up share capital
The amount paid in respect of the issue of shares in a limited company.

Capital employed
The total amount of funds used by a firm and invested in the assets, less the short-term liabilities, of the business.

Corporation tax
The taxation levied by the Inland Revenue on the profits of limited companies.

Cost of production
The costs incurred in the production process of a manufacturing firm. This excludes those costs associated with both administrative and the selling and distributing functions.

Creditors
Amounts owing for goods and services purchased on credit terms.

Current assets
Those assets that are expected to be used during the next year. They include all stocks, debtors and cash.

Current liabilities
Those liabilities that are expected to be settled during the next year. They include creditors, taxation and dividends due, and bank overdrafts.

Debenture
A term used to describe fixed interest loan capital.

Debt
The loan capital of a business.

Debtors
Amounts owing by customers for goods purchased on credit terms.

Depreciation
An estimate of the amount of reduction in the value of an asset due to either use or the passage of time.

Directors
Managers appointed by the shareholders of a limited company to conduct the affairs of the company.

Distributive costs (Selling and distribution costs)
Those costs incurred by a business in connection with its sales and distribution.

Dividends
Payments to the shareholders of a limited company that are dependant on the amount of profit.

Doubtful debts
Amounts owing by customers, in respect of credit sales, which are considered unlikely to be settled in full.

Earnings
A term used to describe the 'profits after tax' of a company. This amount can be distributed as dividend to the shareholders and is considered to have been 'earned' by their capital in the company.

Equity
A term used to describe the shareholders' funds of a limited company.

Final dividend
The payment of a dividend at the financial year end of a company, after taking into account any interim dividends paid during the year.

Finished goods stocks
Manufactured products ready for resale and goods purchased ready for resale.

Fixed assets (Tangible assets)
Those assets that are considered to have a useful life in excess of one year.

FRS (Financial Reporting Standard)
The successor to SSAPs which are no longer issued, but which remain in force until superseded by an FRS.

Goodwill
The premium paid on the purchase of a business that is in excess of the 'book' value of the net assets in the vendor's balance sheet.

Government stocks
Financial instruments issued by the British government on which a fixed rate of interest is paid. These may be issued for a fixed period of time or 'undated', i.e. never to be repaid, e.g. war loan.

Interim dividend
A payment, made half yearly or quarterly, to the shareholders, on account of the annual dividend.

Lenders
Individuals, banks and other financial institutions that have advanced funds to a business, either with or without security, on which interest is to be paid.

Liabilities
Amounts owing by the business. They will include moneys owing for goods and services purchased on credit (*creditors*), bank loans and overdrafts, hire purchase and lease payments due, unpaid taxation, outstanding dividends due to shareholders, as well as longer term loans.

Liquidity
A term used to describe the financial state of a business. A 'liquid' business is one that has a surplus of 'cash' assets, when compared with its immediate liabilities.

Loan capital
Funds borrowed by businesses, either with or without the security of the assets, on which interest is to be paid and which is repayable at a date in the future.

Management accounting
Those accounting processes concerned with the provision of accounting information to management for planning and control purposes.

Net assets employed
Another term to describe the capital employed of a business.

Net current assets
The deduction of current liabilities from current assets. They are also described as 'working capital'.

Oncost
See *Overheads*.

Operating costs
Those costs incurred in the day-to-day operations of a business.

Operating profit
The amount available from the sales income of a business, for a period, after deducting all operating expenses (costs), excluding interest on any loan capital.

Ordinary shareholders
The members of a limited company that hold shares in the company.

Overheads
The expenses incurred in the operation of a business. These exclude the cost of the goods made or purchased for resale. Also known as oncost.

Preference shares (Preference capital)
Share capital of a limited company which pays a fixed rate of dividend. This class of share capital can be redeemed by the company. It is sometimes classed as loan capital because of these characteristics.

Product costs (Product costing)
The determination of the cost(s) of the range of products produced by a business.

Production overheads (Production oncost)
Those annual costs associated with the production functions of a manufacturing business.

Reserves
The undistributed profits of a limited company. These are the profits of the company that have been earned, but not distributed as dividends to the shareholders, and which have been re-invested in the assets of the company. The amount of reserves is shown in the shareholders' funds section of the balance sheet.

Revaluation reserve
The value placed on the assets of a business, usually the properties, over and above the original cost. It is entered in the 'shareholders' funds' section of a balance sheet and represents the value of the increase arising due to the ownership of the asset.

Revenues
The sales income of the business.

Selling and distribution overheads (Selling and distribution oncost)
Those expenses incurred in respect of the selling and distributive functions of a business.

Share capital (Ordinary share capital)
Capital of the company which pays dividends to the holders depending on the amount of profit available. It is the last class of capital to be repaid in the event of a company failure. For this reason it is known as the 'risk' capital of the company. It is also referred to as the 'equity' capital. There can be more than one type of ordinary share.

Share premium (Share premium account)
An amount paid for the purchase of a share from a company above its nominal, or 'face', value.

Shareholders
Investors in the ordinary shares of a limited company.

SSAP (Statement of Standard Accounting Practice)
Regulations concerning the treatment of accounting practice in the preparation of annual financial reports laid down by the accounting authorities. All members of the accounting profession are required to conform to these standards.

Solvency
A surplus of assets over liabilities.

Stocks
These include raw material stocks for manufacturing purposes' work-in-progress which is partly completed manufactured goods, and finished goods for resale.

Work-in-progress
Partly completed manufactured goods.

Working capital

A term used to describe the 'net current assets' of a business. These are the current assets less the current liabilities. In this context 'current' means less than one year.

Index

formulae 4 depreciation: $\dfrac{\text{cost} - \text{residual value}}{\text{estimated life}}$

capital sources are: own share holders and loans
near money.

working capital: $\dfrac{\text{current assets}}{\text{creditors due :}}$
in year

Gross profit margin = $\dfrac{\text{gross profit} \times 100}{\text{turnover}}$ } Profitab
} ratios

Liquidit ratios: If businesses wished to
measure extent to which its
assets could be quickly turned into
cash.

Assets: fixed: Purpose of providing service to
business
current, cash, stock, debtors,
short term investments

liabilities: to transfer economic benefit as a
result of a past transaction.